MW01690657

Cheers!

Susan Fletcher

The Traveling Gourmets

Turtleback Farm Inn
COOKBOOK

By

Denise and Michael Shumway

with

Susan and Bill Fletcher

Edited by

Susan Crabbe Fletcher

Turtleback Farm Inn

Eastsound, WA 98245

Photo Credits:
Front cover food photo ©
by
Michael Skott

Inn photo
by
Jeffrey P. Buchner

Back cover photos
by
Friends

Second Printing 1993.
Second Edition 1998.
Third Edition 2007.
ISBN# 978-0-9663218-6-9

Manufactured in the United States of America
Printed by BookMasters, Inc., Ashland, Ohio

Turtleback Farm Inn
1981 Crow Valley Road
Eastsound, WA 98245
(800) 376-4914 ❖ (360) 376-4914
www.turtlebackinn.com

Dedication

For all of those who have slept in the shadow of
Turtleback Mountain.
- Susan and Bill

To all of those who have shown us
that life is to be celebrated.
- Denise and Michael

To Denise and Michael Shumway

Over a decade and a half ago, this industrious young couple took a chance to create a cookbook for our Inn. They did this on their own time and at their expense. They had a vision of creating a series of books from small Inns and B & B's in the Northwest. They called themselves *The Traveling Gourmets*.

Ours was the only book that was enthusiastically promoted and distributed. This will be the third printing. When the Shumways moved from Orcas Island some years ago to Boise, Idaho, Bill and I bought the rights to their creation. Denise is now a school principal and Michael handles all the computer needs for a large real estate brokerage. They are happily involved in their lives and professions.

We are deeply indebted to their vision and their desire to do something a little different. Our book/their book has sold 1000s of copies and is in kitchens all over the world. Although expanded and corrected in this latest edition, the idea of having a user friendly kitchen helper remains the same.

THANK YOU, YET AGAIN, DENISE & MICHAEL

It was your ideas behind it all!

WE ALSO DEDICATE THIS NEW EDITION TO OUR GENTLE READERS IN HOPES THAT THIS WILL FIND A SPECIAL PLACE IN YOUR KITCHEN LIBRARY

Contents

Preface

It has been ten years since the idea of the Turtleback Farm Inn cookbook was conceived. In that ten years, many hundreds of people have visited the Inn and enjoyed the peacefulness of the island. Many people take part of the experience away with them in the form of this cookbook. To meet the demand, reprints have been necessary. Previous reprints, however, have not reflected the changes that have taken place at the Inn and on the island since the book's inception. Susan felt strongly that the original book captured the Turtleback experience, so she was reluctant to change it. She wanted to make the changes needed to reflect events that have taken place without changing the essence of the book. Further, she had accumulated new recipes which her guests were telling her they wanted to share. Thus the second edition of this book was born.

Although recipes and information have been added, this edition of the cookbook has some sections that are much like the last edition. However, some sections have been updated to reflect changes that have taken place on Orcas Island and at Turtleback Farm Inn. Like most places, Orcas is affected by the ongoing nature of people's lives, but unlike some places, the island has managed to retain an underlying spirit that does not seem to change with its residents. Although time marches on there as anywhere, a very important aspect of island life is how time seems to stand still. In the increasingly frantic pace of life, the Fletchers feel much of what Turtleback Farm has to offer the traveler is a serene and peaceful experience free from the interruptions of modern life; time to read, wander, explore and enjoy the lush peacefulness of the tranquil surroundings. We hope that you have experienced the spirit of Orcas and that the new edition of this book helps to capture it for you.

The traveler was active, he went strenuously in search of people, of adventure, of experience. The tourist is passive; he expects interesting things to happen to him. He goes "sight seeing."

Daniel J. Boorstin, The Image

Food, people and philosophy go well together, as any good dinner party will confirm. One feeds the body; all three nourish the soul. This book is a letter about our travels and the food, people and philosophy we have discovered along the way.

Michael and I call ourselves traveling gourmets. Between us, we have spent 20 years in the food industry. In that time we have lived and traveled over much of the United States. We do not refer to ourselves as gourmets, however, because of the length of time we have spent preparing and enjoying food. Nor does the adjective traveling mean to suggest that we are promoting tourism. If we promote anything, it is that life should be a pleasurable experience guided by education, open-mindedness, awareness and cultural exploration. We feel the word gourmet refers to more than an appreciation of food and wine. It can also refer to an appreciation of life.

Much of my approach to life comes from my uncle Ralph. Leaving home to travel at age sixteen, Ralph is still a wanderer 50 years later. His perspective is a little different from that of most people. He says that being a traveler is how life is meant to be lived; always observing, seeking out new places and ideas, balancing security and roots with adaptability and growth. He loves change. Each new location has a unique personality to him. He expects every place and everyone to be different, and he likes it that way. He is filled with stories of adventure and possesses the wisdom of an open mind.

Not everyone agrees with Ralph's lifestyle, but to us, he is something of a hero. Michael and I do our best to live as he taught us. We face the road with broad-mindedness. When beseiged by the unexpected, we remember that he told us we would rarely experience what we anticipated. But he also said that if we anticipate surprises, life will seldom disappoint us. We welcome the changes people and places bring us. The experiences we have far outlive our travels.

Food, culture and lifestyle are inter-related. All are best when varied, nourishing, explored and savored. This is the point of view we present to you.

In these pages, you will meet some of the people who have broadened us along the way with the food and ideas they have shared. We hope you find a good meal in these pages. And that it feeds you all over.

Orcas Island is a great place to take a fresh look at life. The people who live there are like most Northwesterners; friendly yet private, easy going yet hard working, independent and collectively protective of their environment. But there is a uniqueness about the islanders as well.

Certainly they are influenced by their environment. The landscape is beautiful enough to melt hearts and inspire artists. With its watery surroundings, gently rolling hills, pastoral valleys, huge stands of emerald trees and the clean air tinged with pine and sea breezes, the island feels primal, untouched by the ravages of modern civilization.

Articles written about the island often compare it and its people to some long lost time of simplicity. We found something beyond that. There is the feeling that the people who live there have taken the best of the past, its simple purity, and mixed it with the best of the new, an open-minded worldliness. The people of Orcas Island are not like the old man who, when asked on his hundredth birthday about the changes he had seen, responded, "I was agin every one of 'em." But they will question a suggested change, turn it over for observation and ask what the long term consequences will be.

These people are an eclectic bunch; former CEO's, professional artists and dancers, writers, wanderers, retirees from various professional persuasions, some rich, some poor. Even though there is only one school on the island, with a kindergarten through high school population of less than 500, we found more informed and knowledgeable people there than in some towns with much larger populations. Talent abounds everywhere and the person waiting on your table or fixing your car may have expertise that might surprise you.

If we noticed one thing that seems to set them apart from "the people on the mainland," it is their easy going spirit and respect for one another. If you bring your city thinking with you and roar along the winding country road on someone's bumper, they will simply pull over and let you pass. Only a friendly wave will follow you. Most of these people seem to happily lack a "killer instinct." If you go into a restaurant expecting to buzz through as if you were at a hamburger chain, the staff may quietly remind you that life is a little easier here and that fresh meals made from scratch take longer than fast food duplication.

We suspect that if a survey was taken it would show many islanders view work as much as a means of self expression as anything else. And, like in most small towns, we experienced several examples of residents treating each other like family. There is the same rallying to support someone in need, the same open disagreement on issues big and small.

Part of what we appreciated about Orcas Island was its sense of community. We think when people talk about the good old days, they are not just missing a time with less pollution and stress. People long for this feeling of community; the caring about neighbors, acceptance of individuality and a feeling of safety. And we feel people miss living in communities where their voice can be heard and where they make a difference. It is our guess this is why there is an exodus going on in the United States right now, the so-called fifth migration, an exodus out of the suburbs and into small country communities. The challenge is to do what has thus far succeeded on Orcas Island and a handful of other communities around the country. That approach is a blending of the best of the old with the best of the new and an acceptance of individual lifestyles. Orcas Island hopefully is not a place that time forgot, but rather a glimpse of where we as a society might be headed.

Bill and Susan Fletcher, the owners of Turtleback Farm Inn, are wonderful examples of the people who live on Orcas Island. They, like many people who find the island, were not looking for it. San Francisco Bay area residents, their original intent was to find a summer place. A tip from a friend lead them to the island. Once they arrived, plans changed.

A local real estate agent showed them a farmhouse on an 80 acre parcel of land. The original building was 85 years old and in great need of repair. In the recent past it had been used as a haybarn. A beautiful contemporary house on the back side of the parcel was the owner's home. Her husband, who had designed the house, had recently died. Not wanting to divide the land, she was selling it all or nothing.

Bill and Susan decided it was for them. The issue of how they would make the transition to their new home was a secondary concern. The decision was one from the heart, like that of many island residents. They would move to the island, then decide, once they got there, how to make a go of it.

The idea of transforming the old farmhouse into an inn presented itself weeks later. Against the backdrop of Turtleback mountain, the farm, with its gently, cascading emerald hills, six tranquil ponds, meadows, trees and flowers, created a place of breathtaking beauty and simplicity. The best of the old had survived on the farm. With the light mist in the mornings and the gentle afternoon sunshine, the land was a place where Bill and Susan found peace. They felt others might be in need of such a respite as well.

Orcas Islanders, well aware of the rarity of such a special place, guard the beauty of the island and do not take new buildings lightly. Bill and Susan, respecting the natural state of the land, decided to remodel the farmhouse and leave the area as much in its original state as possible. Many people would not have attempted such a project. It required dedication, vision and a willingness to work hard. Bill and Susan have all three. They met with the planning commissioners and builders. The results of their efforts to recreate the warmth and homeyness of the original building paid off. The redesign is spectacular.

On the inn's parlor table is a scrapbook which contains pictures of the remodeling process. Most guests are stunned when they see how the house looked before the transformation. All of the original farmhouse exists within the framework of the inn. Careful planning and design give the inn the peaceful, cozy feeling of a simpler time. Yet there is a clean elegance that speaks well of the present. The inn is a wonderful blend of the natural environment, the practical and the Fletchers' vision.

Bill did much of the redesigning himself. An artist at heart, he exemplifies the same sturdy self-reliance that you see in many islanders. Having worked as a master engraver for the government, Bill's eye for detail shows in careful accents throughout the house. He chose many of the colors and textures that create the inn's warmth. Braided rugs on the well-polished hardwood floors, gentle comfortable lighting and the soft crackle of a fire in the hearth combine to make one feel at home. Yet, the farm-like atmosphere is enhanced by the inn's touches of regional elegance; there are mirrors and crystal doorknobs from Seattle's grand old Savoy Hotel, and deep sinks and beveled bathroom glass from the regal Empress Hotel in Victoria.

Added to the Inn in 1997 is the Orchard House. A separate building set in the apple orchard looking east to Mt. Wollard, this cedar building was designed to resemble a barn. It continues the tradition of fine craftsmanship that is so evident at Turtleback.

Bill's experiences on his grandfather's farm in Virginia contribute to the ambiance at Turtleback. The eggs are gathered from Turtleback chickens. The comforters on the beds are lined with the wool of Turtleback sheep. Homemade jams, made from the farm's orchards, are often served with breakfast. Sitting in the dining room at the inn, we watched the sheep munching across the pasture, the chickens down in the yard scurrying from one curiosity to the next, and the ducks milling about the pond. Memories are rarely sweeter.

We thought that competing with the beauty visible from the dining room windows was no easy task, but Susan, the inn's gourmet cook, does it in stride. The rich aromas and heavenly flavors of Susan's wonderful breakfasts compliment the scenery nicely. Among her favorite recipes are crêpes smothered in island blackberries, cornmeal waffles, ham omelets or her famous homemade granola, which took the blue ribbon at the county fair. They all drew our attention away from the window to our other senses.

Susan reminded us of a younger Katherine Hepburn with her combination of world traveler sophistication and girl next door charm, wit and straightforwardness. The daughter of famed actor Buster Crabbe, she was raised in Hollywood. Her mother and father were a handsome, dashing couple, as attested by the pictures that hang in the inn and her home. The family was close knit. Her parents met when they were teenagers and remained virtually inseparable until his death several years ago. She and her mother often joined her father in various locations around the world. The experiences of travel at a young age show in the ease with which Susan responds to people and the unexpected situations that always arise in life.

In her culinary approach, there is the blending of the best of all possible worlds. Her menus often contain a wonderful mix of dishes. During one meal you might taste a unique combination of down home cooking and French cuisine. Yet the fare is always balanced. She insists on fresh, locally grown produce. She and Bill both appreciate the days when everyone grew their own food.

Susan is generous with her recipes. She had the granola recipe printed and sent out with Christmas cards. And when we asked how she put the zing in her homemade mustard or the pizazz in her Eggs Benedict, she did not hesitate to share. Having done a variety of entertaining in her life, Susan is comfortable preparing many types of dishes.

Although the inn is officially a bed and breakfast, Turtleback has been reserved for weekends by wedding parties. Susan also has done theme dinners for week-end groups. Her credo is that for a meal to be memorable, we must have a few surprises, but enough of the familiar to allow us to invoke trusting appetites. She says it takes flexibility in the kitchen, for one never knows when a little surprise will not turn out as expected. "Always have a back-up plan," she advises. "If you use fresh ingredients creatively, but stay within a menu framework, you can never go too far wrong. Serve the dishes unhesitatingly," she says, "your guests will feel relaxed because of your confidence."

Bill and Susan's confidence definitely influences the atmosphere at the inn. For all the inn's beauty, it was their sense of security which made it easy for us to relax. We felt safe there. Because they live in the house down the hill, we never felt that we had intruded upon their lives. They were always nearby when we needed them; then, they seemed to vanish into the woodwork, leaving us to our privacy and freedom. And although Bill was a country boy and Susan was a city girl, they have created a delightful composite style with the interaction of and respect for their differences.

Bill and Susan do best what all great hosts do - - they made us feel important. And we felt at home at the inn because they are so obviously at home with themselves.

Scrapbook

View of Turtleback Farm Inn from the pasture.

View of the San Juan Islands from Mt. Constitution.

Our room for the night

Spud and a gander discuss who's the boss

Sheep shearing day at the farm

Susan's oven baked pancakes

A couple of the friendly residents of the island

The Inn Parlor

View of Madrona Point from Crescent Beach

The Orchard House

Two bedrooms at Turtleback Farm Inn

Welcome Home Ian!

Tower on Mt. Constitution

Orcas was settled as a farming and fishing community. Turtleback Farm is only one of many remnants of once active farmlands. Among the islands chief crops was fruit. As we walked, biked and drove the island, we saw several still fruitful orchards. There are several ancient orchards, including one at Turtleback, still growing varieties of apples that are all but extinct in other areas of the country. In the fall, the county extension agent brings interested parties to the island to study the trees and sample the unusual fruits.

Another staple crop of the islands was strawberries. Many early settlers earned extra money as strawberry pickers and packers. A scant two blocks from the original ferry dock in Olga is the Artworks. The Artworks, a café and gallery housed in a refurbished strawberry packing house, is a wonderful tribute to local talent and ingenuity. The gallery, a cooperative, displays and sells artwork by island craftpeople. Among the items are pottery, paintings, clothing, candles and ceramics. Far from being the typical gift shop items, these items are useful, elegant and just as the name implies, art, lovingly and skillfully created. We wonder how many other communities have such shops. We think it would be wonderful if other communities replaced the typical displays of ashtrays, drinking glasses and t-shirts with the efforts of its most talented citizens.

To give you an idea of the effort and quality put into these items, there are several hand-crafted pieces of wool clothing available. The wool is from sheep raised and sheared on the island, in several cases by the weavers who use it. These artists are so close to their product that they raise the sheep, then dye and spin the wool themselves.

Another type of art at the Artworks is the food in the café. The fare there is simple; fresh salads, sandwiches, quiches, homemade soups and pies. They are also known for their fresh baked cinnamon rolls. It is a wonderful place to go for a delicious lunch. Like Susan at Turtleback, the craftspeople who run the café make good use of local berries and fruits in their kitchen, and they put much of themselves into what they do.

There are several small organic farms on the island and strawberries are still a favorite crop. Strawberries and apples grow well on Orcas Island, the cool moist climate a natural for these fruits. But another berry has the honors when it comes to proficiency, the blackberry. Himalayan blackberries in the Northwest can almost be compared to Kudzu in the South. These plants grow so fast that islanders who are "blessed" with the vines swear they can watch them grow. There are many jokes and stories, including Indian legends, about the almost indestructible plants. Mostly they describe the fate of those who paused beside the vines, only to find themselves engulfed by them in moments.

In the late summer and early fall, blackberry picking is at its peak. Because the vines grow wild along the roadway, opportunities are plentiful to help yourself to a handful. We observed bicyclists beside the road, picking a fresh fruit snack. As we stopped with them, it brought to mind several old sayings about taking the time to appreciate the simpler things in life.

If you want to pick a few berries, and you might once you see Susan's recipes, there are a few things to remember.

Blackberries vines are feisty plants, not only because they take territory without hesitation, but because they do not willing give up their fruit for the favor of growing on your land. The berries are surrounded by prickly thorns which do not just prick, but grab. If at all possible, wear long sleeves and pants when picking berries. Gloves are also a good idea. And if you do get grabbed, do not pull away quickly, but gently remove the vine, one thorn at a time.

The berries are indeed black and soft when ripe. The deep

crimson and blue ones, though, are too tart to use.

Susan loves to top things with the fresh berries. They add color to a plate, nutrition to the body, and delicious flavor to almost any dish including eggs. Any of the following recipes may be topped with berries, but they are especially good with the crêpes, the granola and the waffles, which are pictured on the cover.

Experts tell us that we're supposed to start each day with a full breakfast. At Turtleback, we make sure that our guests have that opportunity. Because breakfast is what we serve daily, the dishes we offer are tasty and unique without being so unusual that we miss the tastes of the majority of our guests.

Each day we offer at least two juices. Because they're so high in nutritional value, few items can serve as many needs as fruit and juice. We prefer fresh squeezed orange and pressed apple juices. In the fall, we offer juice from our orchard and when this is not available, we buy local fresh pressed juice.

We also prefer fresh fruits because they are higher in nutritional content and look and taste superior to canned or frozen fruit. What we serve depends on what's in season. In the summer, I prefer melons and berries, including, but not limited to, strawberries, blueberries, raspberries and wild blackberries. I don't doctor the fruit with syrups or sugar. A good piece of ripe fresh fruit should be able to stand on its own. Finding it pref-

I am hesitant to give an exact number of servings with my recipes. Bill and I have raised eight children. Some of our children have large appetites while others have small ones, so I know only too well how serving sizes can vary. Please see the number of servings as a general guideline.

-Susan

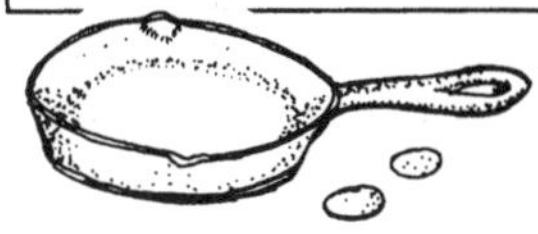

erable to allow guests to sweeten the fruit to their tastes, I make sure there is honey or raw sugar on the table. In the fall, I bake apples and make applesauce, pear- sauce and stewed ginger rhubarb. Many people are surprised to learn how tasty rhubarb is when served this way.

If I find I need to treat the fruit with a sauce to perk up the flavor, I use my favorite fresh fruit sauce. This is especially good on melon and can be used on fruit served for dessert.

Fresh Fruit Sauce

This recipe may be made omitting the rum.

1/3 cup water
1 teaspoon lemon or lime zest
1/4 cup lemon or lime juice
1/2 cup honey or sweeten with honey to taste
1/2 cup light rum

> Bring all ingredients except the rum to a boil, then simmer for 5 minutes. Cool.
> Add the rum. Refrigerate and use as needed.

Being in the hospitality industry is like being a parent. You cannot be a part-time parent; nor can you be a part-time innkeeper. It is a very intense business. People have expectations. You must be genuinely interested in their comfort.
-Susan

Zest is the outer rind or colored part of the citrus fruits. It contains oils which can enhance the flavor of many dishes. Zest can be removed with a vegetable peeler or julienned with a sharp knife. A zester is a tool that is made to remove long even strings of peel easily. Be sure to remove only the thinnest layer of rind. The white pith contains wonderful nutrients, but is bitter to the taste.

Baked Apples

This may be offered for dessert, served with vanilla ice cream and cinnamon to taste.

6 baking apples, cored but not cut all the way through
3 teaspoons butter, melted
1 1/2 cups brown sugar
3/4 cup water
3/4 cup orange juice
1/2 cup raisins
1/2 cup walnuts
lemon juice
cinnamon
nutmeg
light cream

>Preheat oven to 350°.
>Slice the apples and layer them in a baking dish.
>Mix all remaining ingredients in a separate dish and pour over the sliced apples.
>Bake at 350° for 30 to 45 minutes or until soft when pierced with a fork.
>Serve warm with a pitcher of cream, or with the cinnamon cream on page 31.
Serves 6.

The best apples grown in Western Washington for cooking are: Gravenstein, Summerred, Mutsu, Jonagold and Melrose. Some of the most popular varieties of apples sold in the United States are not grown here, but shipped from overseas.

The average amount of distance a food in the United States travels before it is eaten is 1300 miles.

An apple a day keeps the doctor away.
American Proverb

So cheek to cheek and jaw to jaw,
We sucked the cider through a straw.
Pretty soon the straw did slip;
I sucked sweet cider from her lip.
That's how I got me a mother-in-law,
From sucking cider through a straw.

Applesauce Bread Pudding

This "dessert for breakfast" is great with bacon or ham.

8 slices of raisin bread
1/2 cup softened butter
1/2 cup raisins
2 teaspoons cinnamon
1 teaspoon nutmeg
1/2 cup brown or granulated sugar
1 1/2 teaspoons vanilla extract
3 cups milk
4 eggs
1 cup applesauce, preferably homemade
light or whipped cream

>Preheat oven to 350°.
>Spread bread with butter and sauté on both sides until lightly toasted.
>Cut slices into quarters. Fit into a buttered 9 inch X 13 inch baking dish.
>Spread applesauce on top. Mix the sugar and spices and sprinkle on top, then spread the raisins on top of the sugar-spice mixture.
>In a separate bowl blend milk, eggs and vanilla.
>Pour milk mixture over other ingredients in baking dish.
>Bake at 350° for 30-35 minutes. The pudding should be puffed and nicely browned.
>Serve warm with light or whipped cream.
Serves 6.

Stewed Ginger Rhubarb

12 cups young rhubarb, sliced and trimmed
1 cup dark brown sugar
1 Tablespoon peeled, finely chopped ginger
1 1/2 teaspoons vanilla

>The night before you want to serve this dish, fill a cooking pot with the sliced rhubarb. Rhubarb contains a lot of water and, if it is allowed to sit a few hours, will make its own cooking liquid.

>When ready to cook, add 1/2 cup brown sugar and ginger.

>Bring slowly to a boil over low heat. Simmer for 10 minutes and then allow to cool.

>Add the vanilla and additional sugar as needed. Serve warm or cool.

Serves 4.

Green and Orange Compote

Occasionally, a guest will graciously share a personal recipe with me. This one was sent to me by Jeannie McMacken, who came to the inn on her honeymoon. It can be made up to 2 days ahead.

2 cups apple juice
3 cinnamon sticks
8 cloves
1 cup fresh orange juice
4 Granny Smith apples, cut into 1/2 inch pieces
2 cups seedless green grapes, halved
8 navel oranges, sectioned
8 kiwis, peeled and cut into 2 inch pieces

Rhubarb leaves are inedible. Be sure to trim the stalks before cooking.

-Susan

Citrus isn't the only good source of vitamin C. Other excellent sources are: peppers, broccoli, cabbage, brussels sprouts, greens, honeydew melons, cantaloupe, mangos, papaya and strawberries. Vitamin C is heat sensitive, so when cooking any of the vegetables listed above always expose them to heat as short a time as possible to reduce vitamin loss.

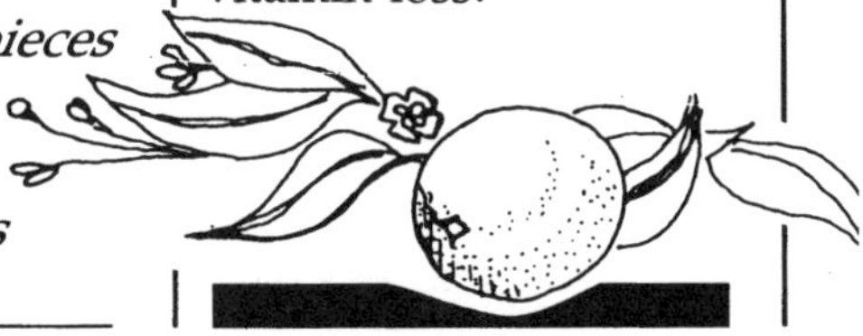

After our guests finish their fruit and cereal, we serve a main course. Each morning of a guest's stay, a different dish will be offered accompanied by either ham, bacon or sausage. As our guests check in, we always ask if they have any food allergies and whether or not they would like breakfast meat with their meal. Initially this was not a part of our check-in routine, but we shortly found that it is important to know of any dietary preferences or problems, just as you would want to know when you have guests in your home. We really did not need to know their car license number.

-Susan

Cup for cup, yogurt provides more calcium than milk.

>Bring apple juice to a boil with the cinnamon and cloves. Simmer for 15 minutes. Cool.
>Add orange juice and strain.
>Stir in all fruit and chill. Cover until ready to serve. Stores best in a glass bowl.
Serves 8-10.

Fruit Butter

1 Tablespoon concentrated orange juice
1/2 teaspoon grated orange rind
1/4 pound butter
honey

> Blend orange juice, orange rind, and butter together.
> Add honey to taste.

Banana Cream for Fresh Fruit

This topping goes well with melons, pineapple and apples and can be used as a topping for pound cake.

3 ripe bananas
2 Tablespoons brown sugar
1 Tablespoon honey
pinch of freshly grated nutmeg
1 cup cream
1 Tablespoon brandy or 1 1/2 teaspoon vanilla

> Mash together bananas, sugar, honey and nutmeg until smooth.
> Whip cream with brandy or vanilla.
> Fold bananas into cream.

Cinnamon Cream

This one is especially good with peaches, pears or apricots.

3 ounces cream cheese, softened
2 Tablespoons powdered sugar
1/2 to 3/4 teaspoon cinnamon
1/2 teaspoon vanilla
1 cup cream

> Blend together cream cheese, sugar, cinnamon, and vanilla.
> Whip cream.
> Gently fold the cream cheese mixture into the whipped cream.
> Spoon over fresh fruit and serve.

If diners have hesitations about alcohol being included in a recipe it can be omitted and vanilla can be substituted with good success.

- Susan

Savory Applesauce

2 cups applesauce, preferably homemade
3 Tablespoons butter
1/2 cup currants
1 1/2 Tablespoon lemon juice
1/2 cup firmly packed brown sugar
1/4 teaspoon each - cinnamon, nutmeg, cloves and allspice

> Cook over low flame until currants are plumped and flavors blended.
> Serve warm or cool.

A good piece of fruit will be heavy for its size. When checking for ripeness, look for fruit that yields slightly to gentle pressure while still feeling firm.

-Susan

Earlier in my cooking career I always cooked with butter. Lately, however, I use olive oil almost exclusively at lunch and dinner. At breakfast I still use butter and/or margarine.

-Susan

We are what we repeatedly do. Excellence, then, is not an act, but a habit.

- Aristotle

Turtleback Farm Granola

Turtleback Farm Inn Granola is always available. We serve it everyday along with the fruit and juice. Many types of granola that are mass produced are too full of sugars and tropical oils. That's unfortunate, because it can be a very healthful food if prepared right. The taste of this granola stands alone, but we serve it with raisins and yogurt on the side. This dresses it up as well as adds further nutritional value.

4 cups rolled oats
3 cups whole wheat flour
1 cup white flour (unbleached)
1 cup shredded coconut
1 cup chopped nuts
1 cup wheat germ
1/2 cup cornmeal
1 cup oil
1 Tablespoon honey
1 cup warm water
1 Tablespoon salt (may be omitted)

>Mix all ingredients well and spread into two 9 inch X 12 inch pans.
>Bake at 300°, stirring often to prevent scorching, approximately 60 - 90 minutes or until nicely browned.

Spiced Pancakes

Although I have listed this recipe with wheat and white flours, any combination of flour, oats, or buckwheat can be used, as long as the total equals 2 cups. Naturally the way the combination works depends on what you use. I have successfully made these pancakes with rice and oat flour because the guest was very allergic to wheat.

---

3 eggs separated
2 cups buttermilk
1/2 cup melted butter
1 cup whole wheat flour
1 cup unbleached white flour
2 Tablespoons sugar
2 teaspoons baking powder
1/2 teaspoon soda
1/2 teaspoon salt
1/2 teaspoon each - cinnamon, nutmeg, allspice

> Beat egg whites until they hold stiff but not dry peaks.
> In a separate bowl, mix together egg yolks, buttermilk and melted butter. Fold in all remaining ingredients, except the egg whites. When all ingredients are well mixed, fold in egg whites.
> Bake on a hot griddle.
> Serve with bacon and savory applesauce.

Crêpes

Crêpes are wonderful because they can be used in a variety of ways, both sweet and savory. You can fill them with chicken or tuna for lunch or dinner. (Recipes for these fillings are on page 99.)

At the inn, I serve at least two crêpes per

Waffles stick to the grids of your waffle iron because of carbon buildup. The more sugar in your recipe, the more carbon buildup on your grids. To keep the iron seasoned but stick free, use a sparing amount of sugar in the batter.

The lightness of waffles depends on the airiness of the batter after the egg whites have been added. For best results take 1/4 of the beaten egg whites and stir into the batter then pile the rest of the whites on top of the batter, gently folding them in.

-Susan

Some batters can be made ahead and stored in the refrigerator. For those whose mornings tend to be rushed, this is a great way to have a nutritious breakfast. Make a couple of batters on Sunday, one for muffins and one for oven baked pancakes, then your fresh breakfast can be cooking while you do other things. The exceptions to this suggestion are batters which contain baking powder.

-Susan

Ideally, crêpe batter should sit 2 to 3 hours before it is used. In all honesty, I have raced into the kitchen, blended up the batter and had crêpes cooked and on the table in a matter of minutes.

-Susan

person and offer seconds. Some of our children can eat four or five without batting an eye. When serving them for breakfast, I top them with the berry sauce (recipe on this page) and a dollop of sour cream or yogurt.

3 eggs
1 cup milk
1 cup unbleached white flour
2 Tablespoons melted butter

>Mix all ingredients well in a blender and let batter sit. Batter should resemble heavy cream.
>Heat skillet over medium high heat. I use a 10 inch silverstone, sloping sided sauté pan. Add a little butter only before cooking the first crêpe. After the initial crêpe is cooked, you should not need to add more butter to the pan.
>While tilting the pan, add just enough batter to thinly coat the bottom of the pan.
>Cook until bubbles pop, about 1 minute. Turn over and brown second side.

Makes 8 crêpes.

Fresh Berry Sauce

This sauce can be used for a variety of purposes, including desserts. I list it here for use with crêpes and oven pancakes.

2 Tablespoons butter
3 Tablespoons sugar
1/2 cup orange juice
1 cup berries

>Melt butter in a sauce pan.
>Add remaining ingredients and cook over medium heat until berries are soft.

If fresh or frozen berries are not available, an acceptable substitute can be made by substituting fruit jam for the berries and sugar, then heating it with melted butter and orange juice.

Smoked Salmon Torte

This is one of my favorite breakfast dishes, but it can also be served as an appetizer. The filling can be spread on toasted English Muffins or I have used it as a filling for omelettes.

Buckwheat Crêpes

3 eggs
1 cup milk
2/3 cup unbleached white flour
1/3 cup buckwheat flour
2 Tablespoons melted butter
Pinch of salt
1 teaspoon butter (for skillet)

> In a large bowl combine eggs, milk, both flours, melted butter and salt. Whisk until batter is like thick cream.
> Place a 10 inch or 12 inch non-stick skillet over medium high heat. Add 1 teaspoon butter and swirl over bottom of pan. After the first crêpe is done, no additional butter should be needed.
> Pour in enough batter to thinly coat the skillet and cook until bubbles pop and the underside is golden, about 1 minute.

According to *Longevity* magazine, the three most powerful factors to long life that are within your control are:
> Where you live.
> What you eat.
> Whether you exercise.

We use a company in Anacortes to supply our salmon. SeaBear produces a variety of smoked salmon, oysters and mussels. They have a catalog available with a great assortment of smoked fish products and gift items. A current edition is available by calling 1-800-645-3474.
- Susan

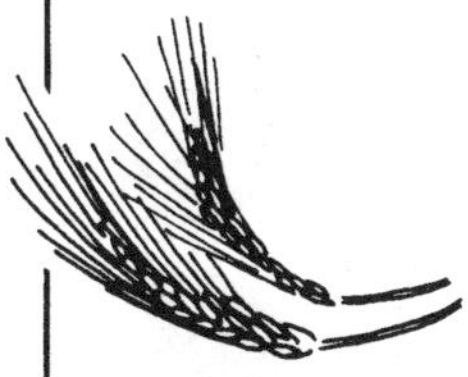

The strongest advice I can give new cooks is to read a recipe all the way through before beginning it. Many times I have made the mistake of racing ahead only to find myself mid-way through a recipe and knee deep in trouble.
-Susan

The word farmer comes from the Latin word for ground, firma. Originally the term was applied to the owner of the land whether or not he worked it. After the 15th century, the term became associated with the one who tilled the soil.

Flip crêpe and cook for an additional 10 to 30 seconds until crêpe is lightly browned. Transfer to a plate and continue making crêpes until all the batter is used. You should have 5 to 6 large crêpes. Keep them covered while you make the filling.

Smoked Salmon Filling

8 ounces cream cheese
1/2 cup sour cream
1/2 pound smoked salmon
1 teaspoon capers, drained
1 1/2 teaspoon Dijon mustard
1 teaspoon minced fresh dill
1 teaspoon lemon juice
additional sour cream and dill springs for garnish

> In a food processor, blend cream cheese, sour cream , mustard, lemon juice and dill. Add salmon and capers and pulse twice to blend, but do not purée.
> To complete the crêpes, spread filling evenly over all but one crêpe, leaving a small amount of filling for garnish. On a serving plate, layer the crêpes on top of one another then top the stack with the remaining crêpe.
>Cut into wedges and top each wedge with small dollops of filling and sour cream. Garnish with dill.

Makes 6-8 servings.

Ricotta Torte with Red Pepper Sauce

Sauce:

1 cup chicken stock
3 red peppers
3 large cloves of garlic - peeled and minced
2 Tablespoons finely chopped onion
1/4 cup sliced mushrooms
2 Tablespoons olive oil
2 Tablespoons butter
2 Tablespoons cream
salt and pepper to taste
basil

> Preheat oven to 425°.
> Bake peppers until skins begin to blacken (about 15 minutes)
> Remove from oven and put into a plastic bag for about 10 minutes.
> Remove from plastic bag and cool, peel and seed.
> Sauté garlic, onions and mushrooms in oil.
> Put garlic, mushrooms, onions and peppers in a processor. Add stock. Process until smooth.
> Transfer to small saucepan. Add butter and simmer for about 5 minutes.
> Add cream, a touch of basil, salt and pepper to taste.
> Keep warm until time to serve.

Filling:

1 bunch spinach, washed, steamed and patted dry
1 cup ricotta cheese
2 Tablespoons finely chopped onion
1/4 cup freshly grated Parmesan cheese

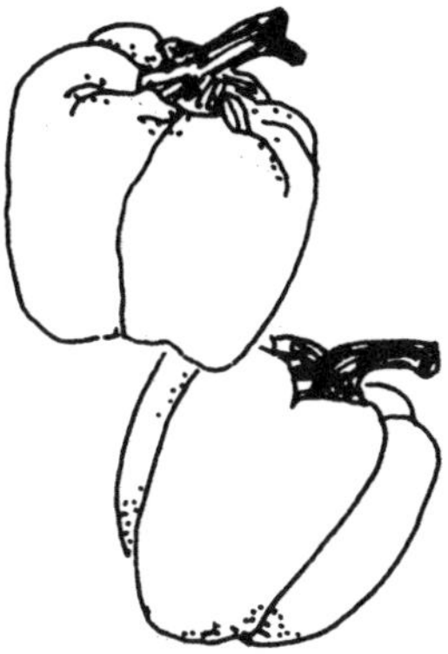

1 egg
1 pinch nutmeg
salt and pepper to taste

> Steam spinach in a minimum amount of water until tender.
> Drain and blend with cheeses, onion, nutmeg, spices and egg in a processor.
> Set aside.

Crêpes:

1 cup milk
2 Tablespoons melted butter
3 eggs
3/4 cups unbleached flour
3 Tablespoons corn meal
pinch salt

> Preheat oven to 325°-350°.
> Blend all the above ingredients in blender, let rest at least 1 hour if possible.
> Lightly coat a 10 inch Teflon skillet with a small amount of butter. While tilting the pan, add just enough batter to thinly coat the bottom, cook until bubbles pop, under 1 minute. Turn and brown the other side.
> Put finished crêpe on a large square of foil.
> Spread 1/5 of the spinach mixture on crêpe. Prepare second crêpe and again spread the filling. Repeat this process until you have 5 filled crêpes and a 6th crêpe as a topping.
> Seal in foil and place in a oven until heated through, about 15 minutes.
>To serve, cut into 6 wedges. Spoon Red Pepper Sauce over wedge and garnish with a dollop of sour cream and fresh oregano or basil leaves.

Spiced Oat Waffles

As a note, all of the waffle recipes are identical in proportions or ratios. Only the raw materials alter to change the flavor.

2 cups buttermilk
3 separated eggs, whites beaten until they hold stiff but not dry peaks
2 Tablespoons honey
1/2 cup melted and cooled butter
1/2 cup all-purpose flour
1/2 cup rolled oaks (not quick cooking)
1 cup whole wheat flour
1 Tablespoon baking powder
1 1/2 teaspoon baking soda
3/4 teaspoon salt
1/4 teaspoon freshly grated nutmeg
1/2 cup toasted and chopped pecans

> Blend buttermilk, egg yolks, honey and melted butter together in a blender, then transfer to a large bowl.
> Mix together the dry ingredients, then add to the buttermilk mixture.
> Fold in the nuts and egg whites.
> Bake on a hot waffle iron according to the manufacturer's directions.
>Serve with pure maple syrup and butter or the fruit butter listed on page 30.

The food that enters the mind must be watched as closely as the food that enters the body.
...Patrick Buchanan

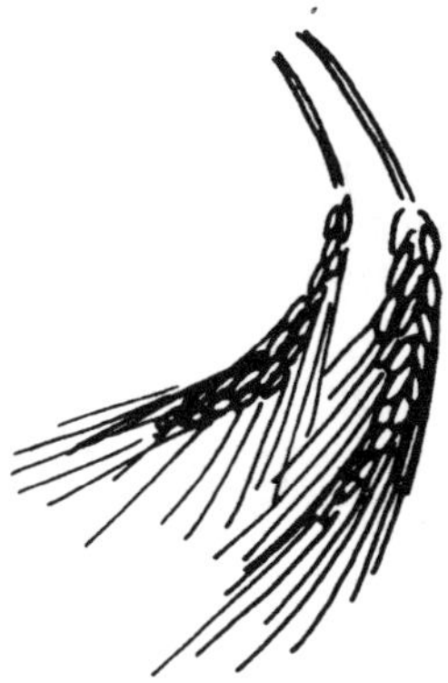

Cooking for people is theatre, as anyone who has worked in a restaurant will tell you. It is an involved performance.
-Susan

Ricotta Pancakes

This is the most requested recipe next to the one for granola. It is so simple that I am almost embarrassed to write it down. In addition to having only a few ingredients, I find that a number of substitutions produce almost the same results. At the risk of having my disguise as a fabulous cook stripped away, I offer the following.

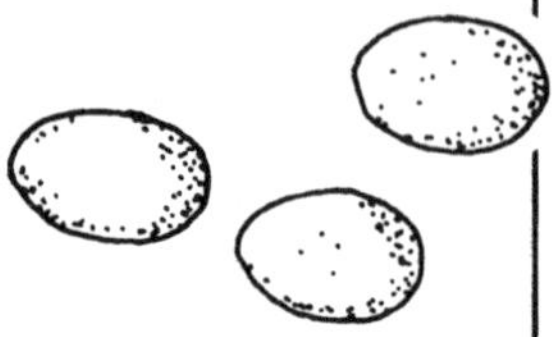

3 eggs, separated
2/3 cup milk
1/2 cup flour
1 teaspoon baking powder
1 cup ricotta cheese

> Beat the egg whites with a pinch of salt until you have stiff, but not dry peaks. Set aside.
> Put the egg yolks in a blender. Add the remaining ingredients and blend together. Place in a bowl.
> Gently fold in the egg whites.
> Cook on a griddle until golden brown.

Because these are so popular, I find guests have two or three servings. Often, no matter how I plan, I run out of batter and sometimes I have used all the ricotta cheese on hand. In desperation I have used sour cream or cottage cheese as a substitute or have left out the cheese altogether and increased the egg by one. All of these scenarios seem to work out. The secret is in the separated eggs. This is also the secret in the ever popular waffle recipes. Separate your eggs and your guests will appreciate the light and tasty pancakes and waffles you serve them.

Pancake batter which is too thick will cause the pancakes to be raw in the center. The secret to well done pancakes is thin batter. Also, some people prefer to add berries after the batter has been poured on the griddle. If your berries are frozen they may leave raw pockets in your pancakes. If the batter is too thin, you have probably left something out.

-Susan

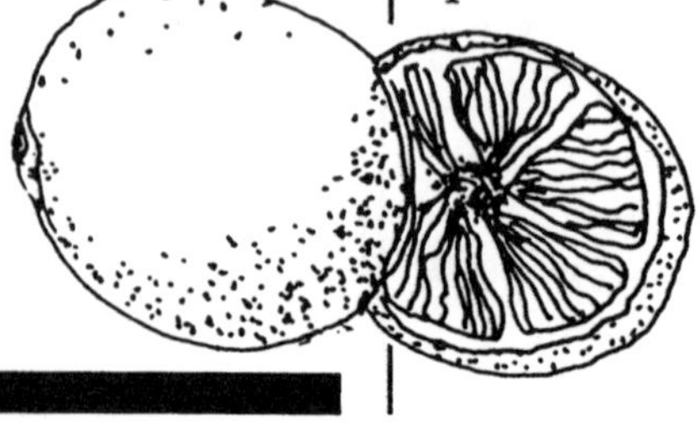

Oven Pancakes

These are called German pancakes and have recently been added to the inn's repertoire. Because the inn's guests do not eat at one time, we cannot make a dish that serves everyone at the same time or that must be served immediately. After a bit of experimentation, I found it best to fill an individual au gratin oven proof dish with about 1/4 inch of batter and bake it in a preheated oven at 425° for about 10 minutes. It is done when you have a puffed up, bowl shaped pancake. Fill the center with fresh fruit and serve warm.

3 eggs
1/2 cup white flour
3/4 cup milk
3 - 4 Tablespoons butter
pinch salt

>Preheat oven to 425°.
>Mix eggs, flour, milk and salt well in a blender.
>Melt 1 Tablespoon of butter in each au gratin dish, then coat the dish with it. Pour 1/4 inch of batter into each warmed dish. Put into oven.
>Bake as above.
Serves 3 - 4.

German pancakes were made famous in the first half of this century by Victor Manca's Seattle restaurant, Manca's. His children called the dish "Dutch Babies." These pancakes can be filled with a variety of things and served for breakfast, brunch, lunch or dinner. It has its roots in Yorkshire pudding.

Sourdough Pancakes or Waffles

The recipe for sourdough starter can be found on page 54. Starter must sit for several days, so be aware of this before starting this recipe.

This is a two part recipe and must be started at least 45 minutes before baking. Letting the batter sit overnight is preferable.

1 cup whole wheat flour
1 cup white flour
1/2 sourdough starter at room temperature
2 cups warmed (100°) buttermilk

>Mix all ingredients. If starting the night before, cover and put into the refrigerator until morning. Let the batter sit covered at room temperature until bubbly.

2 eggs, slightly beaten
1/4 cup milk
1/4 cup oil
2 Tablespoons sugar
1 teaspoon soda
1/2 teaspoon salt

>Mix together and add to the sourdough mixture. Let sit for a few minutes.
>Cook on a hot griddle for pancakes or a pre-heated waffle iron for waffles.
>Serve with butter and warm maple syrup or honey.

Serves 4.

One of the most helpful hints I ever came across was given to me in a cake decorating class. It is a fool-proof preparation for greasing cake pans, bread pans, cookie sheets, muffin tins, etc. Mix together in a food processor; 1 cup flour, 1 cup Crisco and 1 cup oil. Store this in a jar in the refrigerator and use to coat any surface before adding batter to the pan. It really works.

-Susan

Whole Wheat Waffles

This recipe can be adapted for buckwheat or another type of corn waffle. The recipe changes are at the bottom.

1 1/2 cups whole wheat flour
1 1/2 cups unbleached white flour
1 1/2 Tablespoons baking powder
3/4 teaspoon salt
1 1/2 teaspoons soda
2 Tablespoons sugar
6 eggs
3 cups buttermilk
3/4 cup melted butter or margarine
Warmed maple syrup

>Mix together dry ingredients.
>In a blender, mix buttermilk, eggs and melted butter or margarine.
>Add dry ingredients to blender and mix until blended. If batter is too thick, thin with milk.
>Cook on a waffle iron according to manufacturers instructions. Serve with butter and warm maple syrup.
Serves 4.

Buckwheat or Corn Waffles

Use 3/4 cup white flour
3/4 whole wheat flour
3/4 cup buckwheat or cornmeal
The rest of the ingredients remain the same.

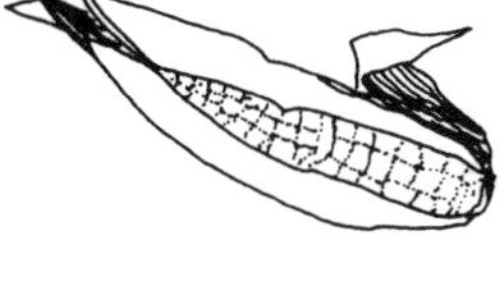

The two most basic and desirable qualities in food are flavor and texture. ...Pierre Franey

A person who counts calories while enjoying a good meal, is like the person who thinks about business while making love. Calories should be counted before a meal is prepared, not while one is in the midst of it.
. . . Shumway's Law

We have always planned one morning a week that we sit in bed, sip coffee and catch up on personal business. Then we like to go out to a Champagne brunch, giving the morning as much of a celebrational atmosphere as possible.

There have been times when we could not afford the meal out, but did not want to spend our morning together in the kitchen cooking and cleaning up. During those times we had breakfast in bed with Champagne, homemade bread, cheese and fruit. We recommend this to anyone who wants to put a little romance into their relationship.

Bill and Susan, on the other hand, are up readying the feast.

Berry Yogurt Pancakes

1/2 cup white flour
1/2 cup whole wheat flour
1 teaspoon baking powder
1/2 teaspoon salt
4 Tablespoons sugar
1/2 teaspoon nutmeg
1 egg
1/2 cup plain yogurt
1/2 cup milk
2 Tablespoons oil
3/4 cup fresh berries, stemmed and sliced (Frozen, unsweetened berries can also be used.)

>Beat together egg, yogurt, milk and oil.
>Mix together dry ingredients, then add to yogurt mixture. Gently fold in berries.
>Cook on a preheated griddle until bubbles form, turn and finish cooking.
>Serve with butter and maple syrup.

Serves 3.

Banana Pancakes with Honey-Nut Butter

1 cup unbleached flour
2 teaspoons baking powder
1/2 teaspoon salt
1/8 teaspoon ground nutmeg
2 Tablespoons sugar
1 egg
1 cup milk
3 Tablespoons oil
1 cup mashed bananas (about 3)
2 teaspoons lemon juice

>Sift together flour, baking powder, salt, nutmeg and sugar.
>Put the milk, egg and oil in a blender and blend at medium speed. Add in the bananas and the lemon juice and blend for a few seconds longer. (You can also slice the bananas and add to the batter as it cooks.)
>Add liquid ingredients to flour mixture and stir until just combined. Batter may be a little lumpy.
>Place greased, seasoned griddle or large cast iron skillet over medium heat until a few drops of water dance on the surface.
>Pour a scant 1/4 cup batter for each cake. Cook on one side until bubbles begin to appear, edges look dry and the cake is fluffy. Then turn and cook the other side until golden brown.
>Serve at once with Honey-Nut butter.
Serves 3.

Honey-Nut Butter

1/2 cup nuts (pecans are my favorite)
3/4 teaspoon orange zest
1/2 cup softened butter
1/2 cup honey

>Spread nuts in a shallow pan and toast in a 350° oven for about 8 minutes. Cool. Chop nuts finely.
>In a food processor, process orange zest and butter until fluffy. Add honey and process until well combined.
>Add nuts and pulse until just blended.
>Serve at room temperature.

What hunger is in relation to food, zest is in relation to life.
...Bertrand Russsell

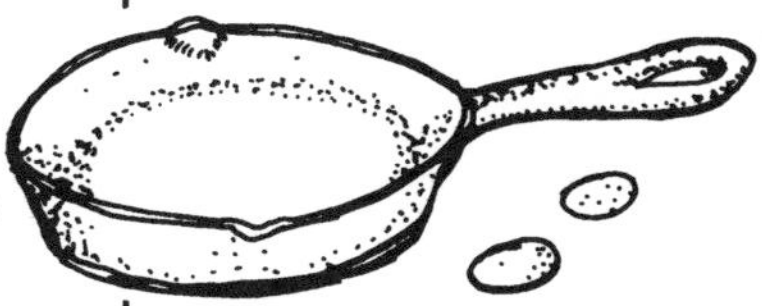

The honey-nut butter may be made ahead, covered and refrigerated.
-Susan

For a different flavor add a teaspoon or two of Grand Marnier or rum to the French toast batter.
-Susan

Northwesterners love their coffee strong. All over Washington state you will find espresso stands which serve a variety of coffees and treats. The standard favorites are; espresso, an extra strong coffee prepared by a special machine through which steam under high pressure is forced; café au lait, equal amounts of strong hot french roast and warmed milk poured into a cup simultaneously; cappuccino , an Italian coffee made by adding a tiny amount of warmed milk and topping with milk foam; mocha, a strong coffee mixed with steamed milk and chocolate. If you do not have an espresso machine you can make café au lait or cappuccino by heating the milk, whipping it in a blender to simulate steamed milk, then adding it to strong brewed coffee. For a mocha, add chocolate to the milk while it is whipping.

Overnight French Toast

A favorite couple who stayed at Turtleback sent me this recipe. A very elegant and rich breakfast, I adapted it because we found it too sweet.

---

8 pieces of homestyle bread, thinly sliced
1/4 cup melted butter
1/2 cup brown sugar
2 Tablespoons molasses
1/2 cup orange juice
5 eggs
1 1/2 cups milk
1 1/2 teaspoons vanilla
1 cup fresh berries
sour cream
1/2 cup walnuts

>Mix butter, sugar, molasses and orange juice. Pour into a 10 inch X 13inch pan. Tilt to cover bottom.
>Cover with 8 pieces of homestyle bread. You may want to double-deck the bread.
>Mix eggs, milk and vanilla in blender.
>Pour the mixture over the bread and refrigerate overnight.
>In the morning, preheat oven to 350°, then bake the mixture, uncovered, for 45 minutes or until nicely puffed and golden.
>Cut into servings and flip over into plate. Top with sour cream, fresh berries and a sprinkling of walnuts.

Serves 4.

Fabulous-Fattening French

This recipe also works well with croissants.

12 slices day old homestyle bread (can be raisin)
1 - 8 ounce package cream cheese, softened with a little milk added
3/4 cup half and half or milk
3 eggs
1/4 cup biscuit mix
1 teaspoon vanilla
apricot jam
oil for cooking
1 cup fresh berries
sour cream or yogurt

>Spread 6 slices of bread with cream cheese and jam. Top with remaining bread slices to make a sandwich.
>In a blender, mix together remaining ingredients and pour into a pie plate.
>Soak sandwiches in batter on both sides until well saturated.
>In a wide frying pan, heat about 1/4 inch oil until medium hot. Fry sandwiches, a couple at a time, until browned and puffy on each side. Drain on a paper towel and keep warm until all are done.
>To serve, cut each sandwich in half, diagonally, and serve garnished with fresh berries and sour cream or yogurt.
Serves 6.

For variety, you may substitute thinly sliced ham and swiss cheese for the cream cheese and jam.
-Susan

We cannot become what we need to be by remaining what we are.
. . . Max De Pree

I prefer raw milk cheddar cheese above all the other cheeses I have tried for cooking. It is not overly colored, has the best flavor and melts smoothly without being too chewy.

-Susan

The world is a book, and those who do not travel read only one page.
-St. Augustine

Texas Sausage Bread

The original recipe for this bread was given to us by a guest from Houston, Texas. We have adapted it a little for use at the inn. I usually accompany the bread with either a boiled or baked egg.

1 pound breakfast sausage (I use Jimmy Dean's or Tarheel Brand)
1 medium onion, diced
1/4 teaspoon Tabasco
1 teaspoon salt
2 Tablespoons chopped parsley
1/2 cup grated Parmesan cheese
1/2 cup grated raw milk cheddar or swiss cheese
3 eggs
2 cups unbleached white flour
1 Tablespoon baking powder
3/4 teaspoon salt
3/4 teaspoon soda
4 Tablespoons salad oil
3/4 teaspoon Dijon mustard
2/3 cup buttermilk
2 Tablespoons milk

> Preheat oven to 375°. Butter a 10 inch pie dish.
> Brown sausage and onion over medium heat in a heavy skillet.
> When the meat is browned, mix in the cheeses, Tabasco, salt, parsley, and 1 egg. Blend well.
> Make a batter by mixing together the flour, baking powder, salt, soda, salad oil, 1 egg, mustard and buttermilk.
> Place 1/2 the mixture in the bottom of the prepared pan. Top with the sausage

mixture. Then spread the rest of the batter over the sausage.

> Mix the remaining egg with the 2 Tablespoons milk. Paint the top of the batter.
> Bake for 25-30 minutes or until puffed and nicely browned.
> Cut into wedges and serve.

Ginger Muffins

These muffins can also be rolled on a floured board and cut with a biscuit cutter.

2 cups flour
1/3 cup brown sugar
2 Tablespoons baking powder
1 teaspoon ginger
1/8 teaspoon cloves
3/4 teaspoon cinnamon
6 Tablespoons butter
1/4 cup milk
1 egg
3 Tablespoons molasses
1 teaspoon vanilla
2/3 cup raisins

> Preheat oven to 375°.
> Whisk together the milk, butter, egg, molasses and vanilla.
> Mix together the dry ingredients, add raisins and fold into the milk mixture until blended. Do not overmix.
> Drop by rounded teaspoons onto a prepared cookie sheet.
> Bake for 25 minutes or until lightly browned.

General Oven Temperatures

Very Slow Oven .... 250° - 300° F.
Slow Oven .... 300° - 325° F.
Moderate Oven .... 325° - 375° F.
Med. Hot Oven .... 375° - 400° F.
Hot Oven .... 400° - 450° F.
Very Hot Oven .... 450° - 500° F.

Good communication is as stimulating as black coffee, and just as hard to sleep after.
. . . Anne Morrow Lindbergh

A warm smile is the universal language of kindness.
- W. A. Ward

Angel Biscuits

1 package active dry yeast
1/4 cup warm water (105°-115°)
2 Tablespoons sugar
3 cups unbleached flour
1 Tablespoon baking powder
1/2 teaspoon salt
1/2 cup butter
1/4 cup milk

>Preheat oven to 375°.
> In a small bowl, sprinkle yeast over water. Stir in the sugar and set aside until bubbly. This takes about 10 minutes.
> In another bowl mix the remaining ingredients, except the milk, with a pastry blender until the mixture resembles coarse crumbs.
> Add the milk and the yeast mixture. Mix lightly until combined.
> Cover dough with a clean cloth and let rise until double in size.
> Turn onto a floured surface, punch down and roll out dough to 1/2 inch thickness. Cut with a 3 inch round cutter into a dozen biscuits.
> Place on a large, greased cookie sheet. Pierce tops a few times with the tines of a fork. Let biscuits rise again until doubled, about 45 minutes.
> Bake for 15 to 18 minutes or until golden brown.
> Serve warm with butter and jelly or honey.

Sesame Corn Muffins

This recipe was given to me by my good friend Jan Helsell.

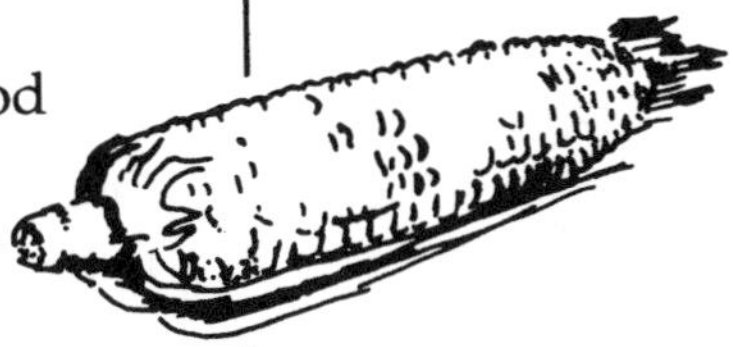

3/4 cup unbleached flour
3/4 cup whole wheat flour
1/2 cup sugar
1 1/2 teaspoons salt
1 1/4 teaspoons baking soda
2 cups cornmeal
1 cup wheat germ
1/2 cup toasted sesame seeds
2 cups buttermilk
3/4 cup melted butter
2 eggs, slightly beaten

>Preheat oven to 350°.
>In a large bowl, sift together flours, sugar, soda and salt. Stir in cornmeal, wheat germ and sesame seeds.
>In a blender, mix buttermilk, butter and eggs on medium speed until thoroughly blended.
>Pour milk mixture into dry ingredients. Blend just until moistened. Do not overmix.
> Pour into greased muffin tins, 2/3 full.
> Bake at 350° for 30 minutes.
Makes 12 muffins.

Love and eggs are best when they are fresh.
...Russian Proverb

To make lighter muffins, place greased tins into the oven for a few minutes before adding the batter.

For easy cleanup, fill a dirty blender part of the way with hot water. Add a drop of detergent, put on the cover and turn it on for a few seconds. Rinse and drain dry.

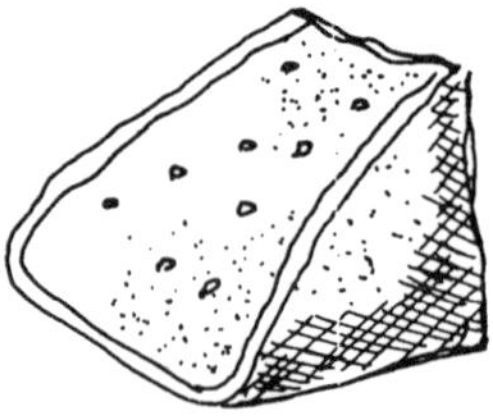

Flowers are a wonderful garnish for egg dishes. Choose edible, pesticide-free unbruised varieties. Some favorites are borage, pansies, primroses (except Chinese primroses), lavender, nasturtiums, roses (petals only) and violets.

Honey-Mustard Cheddar Muffins

One of the best things about breakfast muffins is that you can make enough for several days ahead and always have a quick breakfast.

1 cup unbleached white flour
1 cup whole wheat flour
1/2 teaspoon salt
freshly ground pepper to taste
1 Tablespoon baking powder
1 cup sharp cheddar cheese, grated
1 egg
2 Tablespoons Dijon mustard
3 Tablespoons honey
1 1/4 cups milk
1/4 cup melted butter

> Preheat oven to 400°.
>Combine dry ingredients in a mixing bowl.
>Whisk together the rest of the ingredients and gently, but thoroughly, fold it into the dry ingredients.
> Fill greased muffin tins.
>Bake at 400° for 20 minutes or until done.
Makes 12 muffins.

Sour Cream Coffee Cake

1 cup soft butter
1 cup sugar
3 eggs, beaten
3 cups flour
1 teaspoon vanilla

1 cup sour cream
3 teaspoons baking powder
1 teaspoon soda
1 cup brown sugar
1 1/2 cups nuts, chopped
1 Tablespoon cinnamon
1 teaspoon nutmeg

>Preheat oven to 350°.
>In a bowl, mix together brown sugar, nuts, cinnamon and nutmeg. Set aside to use as topping.
>Cream butter and sugar. Add the eggs, then the flour and mix.
>Stir in vanilla, sour cream, baking powder and soda.
>Spread 1/2 topping into a greased tube pan. Pour 1/2 batter over topping. Spread remaining 1/2 topping over this and then add remaining batter.
>Bake 50 minutes. Let stand 10-15 minutes before serving.

Biscuits

These biscuits are great for breakfast but also make a wonderful picnic bread. They work well for sandwiches if you make them large. To do this, make yourself a biscuit cutter from an empty tuna can. Wash the can thoroughly, being careful of rough edges. This cutter can be used for making English muffins or crumpets.

3 cups unbleached white flour
1 cup whole wheat flour
1/2 cup unsalted butter

Biscuit Ideas

Split them and fill with thin slivered ham, cornichon pickles, a bit of mustard and a few sprouts.

* * *

Split them and fill with softened cream cheese and fresh jam or cream cheese with water cress or cucumber rounds.

* * *

Serve them whole with an assortment of cheeses and fruits.

* * *

Eat them plain with butter and honey.

* * *

While they are still warm spread them with a tablespoon of the following mixture:
1 cup walnuts
1/2 cup marmalade
1/2 cup creamed butter
honey to moisten.

* * *

Split and fill with egg salad.

He that travels much, knows much.
. . . Thomas Fuller

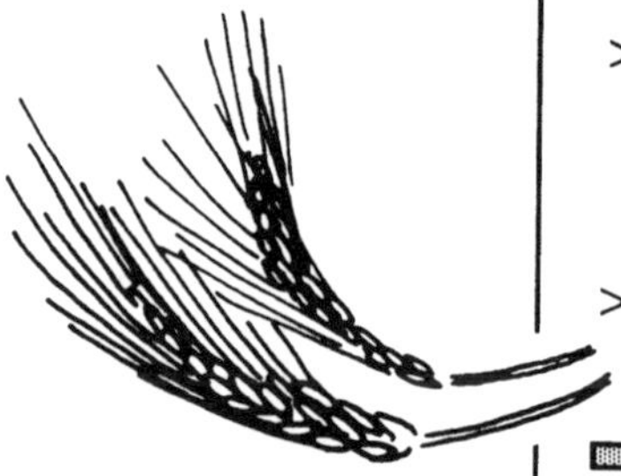

If you accidently scorch the inside of your favorite saucepan, there is a solution. Fill the pan halfway with water, then add ¼ cup of baking soda. Bring the mixture to a boil, then continue to boil until the burned portions loosen and float to the top.

2 Tablespoons baking powder
3/4 teaspoon salt
2 cups heavy cream

>Preheat oven to 375°.
>Process dry ingredients and butter in food processor until it resembles corn meal.
>Pour cream through feed tube and pulse until dough begins to form a ball, this should take about 30 seconds.
>Knead on a lightly floured board about 10 times. Roll out and cut into rounds with a biscuit cutter. Place 1 inch apart on a lightly greased cookie sheet.
>Bake at 375° until puffed and lightly browned. Serve with butter and jam or honey.

Sourdough Starter

Sourdough is a popular bread in the Northwest. Once you have starter available, it is also easy. Starter is not complicated to make, but it does require a few days to become active before you begin to bake with it. All you need is a few simple ingredients and a warm kitchen. My home is usually quite cool, so I don't make starter at home. I have gas ovens at the inn which are perfect for getting starter going.

Once you have starter, you only need to feed it regularly and you'll never need to make a new batch again. Below is the starter recipe. On page 56 is a recipe for bread made with sourdough. On page 42, is a recipe for sourdough pancakes or waffles.

1 cup skim milk
3 Tablespoons plain low-fat yogurt
1 cup unbleached flour

>Heat skim milk to approximately 95°, almost body temperature.
>Remove from heat and stir in yogurt.
>Pour into a 1 1/2 quart glass container. Cover it tightly.
>Let stand in a warm place. (between 80° and 100°, no cooler or hotter.)
>After 24 hours, the mixture should resemble yogurt. If some clear liquid has come to the top, stir it back in; if the liquid is light pink, the milk has broken down. You should throw out the mixture and start again.
>Once your mixture has a yogurt consistency, add the cup of unbleached flour, stir until well blended and cover tightly. Return it to a warm place until it smells good and sour and the surface is all bubbly. This should take 2 to 5 days.

During this time if a clear liquid comes to the top, stir it back in. If the liquid is light pink, discard all but 1/4 cup of the mixture and blend in 1 cup warm skim milk and 1 cup flour. Let it sit again until warm and bubbly.

Your starter is now ready for use. Each time you use some of the mixture, you must replenish your supply. To replenish, you simply stir in equal amounts of warm, 80°-100° skim milk and unbleached white flour. If you do not use your starter regularly, throw half of it away and feed or sweeten it with equal amounts of warm milk and flour. If you do this regularly, every 10 days or so, you will always have active starter on hand.

The tongue of a wise man lieth behind his heart.
Ali Ibn-Abi-Talib

Whole wheat bread does not have a hollow sound when tapped as an indication of being fully baked. White bread does.

-Susan

When buying breads at the market, look for the words whole grain or whole wheat. Wheat flour is equal in nutrition to white flour.

Bread can be baked with their own brown crusts, or they can be glazed. The risen loaves can be brushed with milk or melted butter for a soft crust. For shiny crusts use an egg beaten with a Tablespoon of water.

To simulate the old brick ovens, some people put a pan of water in the bottom of the oven while baking bread. I like to use a squirt bottle filled with water. Squirting the bread a few times during the baking process makes a wonderful loaf with a chewy crust.

-Susan

Classic Sourdough French Bread

Plan ahead if you want to make your own sourdough bread. Because you do not use yeast, but depend on the natural leavening action of the starter, the dough cannot be rushed.

---

2 cups warm water (110°)
1 cup sourdough starter, let it come up to room temperature
4 cups unbleached white flour
2 teaspoons salt
2 teaspoons sugar
2 Tablespoons corn meal
3 cups unbleached white flour

>Mix together 4 cups of the flour, water and the starter. Let it sit covered in a warm corner of your kitchen overnight, or at least 8 hours.

>When bubbly and spongy, stir in the salt, sugar and enough of the remaining flour to make a stiff dough. Knead either by hand or with a machine until smooth and elastic, about 10 minutes. Turn into a greased bowl and let rise until double in bulk, about 2 hours.

>Punch dough down and divide in half. Shape either into two round loaves or two long baguette shaped loaves. Put each one on a cookie sheet sprinkled with a little corn meal. Let rise again until almost doubled.

>Preheat oven to 400°. While oven is heating, slash the tops a couple of times with a sharp razor blade.

>Bake in the middle of the oven for 20 - 25 minutes.

Makes 2 loaves.

French Bread in a Bread Machine

This recipe can be made omitting the sourdough starter if you do not have any. You will still end up with a very tasty fresh bread.

2 1/2 cups unbleached white flour
1/2 cup whole wheat flour
1 1/2 teaspoon yeast
1 1/2 teaspoon salt
1 1/2 cups water
1 Tablespoon sourdough starter
1 teaspoon lemon juice - do not omit this!

> Mix the ingredients according to the directions on your machine.
> At the end of the second kneading, the bread is ready to be hand shaped. Place dough on a lightly floured surface. Cut in half and shape into baguettes or shape the whole piece of dough into one round loaf.
> Slash each loaf with a sharp knife or razor. Glaze with egg white. Place in a draft free place until dough has doubled in size.
> Bake in a preheated 400° oven until deep brown, about 25 - 30 minutes.

Naturally the first step to making French Bread in a machine is to have a bread machine. A thoughtful son gave us one for Christmas and we have found it a treat to have fresh bread from the oven at dinnertime with no hassles. The added calories seem unavoidable because hot bread demands either butter or oil and balsamic vinegar to dip it in. All this aside, I have found that I can make very tasty sourdough bread using the machine to mix and proof the bread. You still must hand shape the loaf and bake it in the oven.

- Susan

Milk is one of many liquids that can be used in bread making, but it plays an important role because of its nutritional value. Many old cookbooks directed the baker to scald fresh milk, because unscalded milk caused soft dough and interfered with the rising process. Pasteurization alters milk chemistry enough to prevent that effect so today few recipes call for scalded milk.

When doubling a baking recipe, do not double the salt.

Turtleback Farm Whole Wheat Bread

6 cups warm water (80°-100°)
6 cups whole wheat flour
2 Tablespoons yeast
2/3 cup dry milk powder
2/3 cup potato flakes
1/2 cup rolled oats
1/2 cup wheat germ
1/2 cup corn meal
2 eggs
2/3 cup oil
2/3 cup honey
3 Tablespoons salt
8 cups whole wheat flour

>Add yeast to water. Mix well until dissolved.
>Add 6 cups whole wheat flour. Mix well.
>Add remaining ingredients and enough of the remaining flour to make a stiff dough. Knead until smooth and non-sticky, about 7 to 10 minutes.
>Turn into a greased bowl and let rise until double in bulk. (I use a heavy duty mixer with a dough hook. For the first rising I leave the dough in the bowl to rise, covering it with a towel. When it has doubled, I turn on the motor and knead it a bit more with the dough hook.) If you do not use this method after the dough has risen, punch down and knead again.
>Divide into loaves. Put dough seam side down in greased bread pans and let rise again about 45 - 60 minutes.
>Preheat oven to 375°. Bake for 35 - 45 minutes, or until the bottom of the loaf is golden.
Makes 2 loaves.

Turtleback Farm Whole Bran Muffins

I loved bran muffins even before the great bran debate. These are so tasty, they're worth eating for the flavor alone. And if they are good for you, so much the better. These are excellent with coffee or tea breaks. And for a light lunch, just add a slice of ham or some cream cheese.

> The batter for Whole Bran Muffins will store well for up to 8 weeks if placed in a sealed container in the refrigerator.
> -Susan

1 cup 100% bran cereal
1 cup boiling water
1/2 to 3/4 cup honey or brown sugar, depending on taste
1/2 cup shortening
2 well beaten eggs
2 1/2 cups flour
2 1/2 teaspoons soda
1/2 teaspoon salt
2 cups buttermilk
1 cup All-Bran cereal
1 cup granola (Turtleback Farm Inn if you have it)
Optional: 1 cup raisins and/or 1 cup walnuts

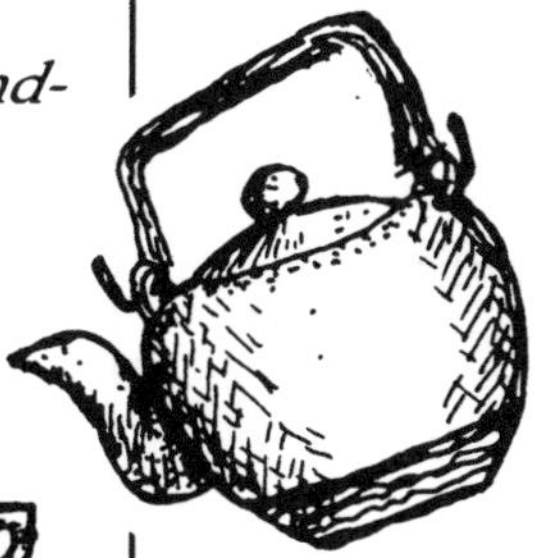

>Preheat oven to 375°.
>Combine 100% Bran and water, allow to cool.
>Cream sugar or honey and shortening. Add eggs to the shortening mixture. Then add this mixture to the bran and water.
>Sift dry ingredients together. Add to the bran mixture in small batches, alternating with buttermilk.
>Add All-Bran and granola. At this point the raisins or walnuts can be added if you are using them.
>Fill greased muffin tins 2/3 full. Bake at 375° for 12-15 minutes.

Makes 18 muffins.

Beyond Mexican Eggs

This is basically the same recipe, but additional ingredients give the dish a different spin. Brown chopped ham or sausage with chopped onion. Drain well and crumble. Add this to the chilies and cheese, pour the milk/egg mixture over all, and bake as for Mexican Eggs.

- Susan

Mexican Eggs

I usually serve these with corn muffins and ham. When allowed to cool and cut into squares, they're also great for appetizers.

1 *-4 ounce can whole Ortega chilies*
1 pound grated raw milk cheddar
1 1/2 cups milk
5 large eggs
1 Tablespoon flour
1 teaspoon dijon mustard

> Preheat oven to 375°.
> Butter the bottom of a 10 inch glass pie pan, or a 9 inch x 13 inch rectangular one if you want to cut into squares.
> Arrange chilies on the bottom of the pan and top with grated cheese.
> Blend remaining ingredients in a blender and pour over cheese and chilies.
> Bake at 375° for 45 minutes or until puffed and golden. Serve with a dollop of sour cream, a sprig of fresh cilantro and a slice of tomato on top. Offer fresh salsa on the side.

Serves 6.

Fresh Salsa

Salsa adds zip to any egg dish, be it simple scrambled eggs or a breakfast quiche. This is my favorite salsa recipe.

3 or 4 ripe tomatoes, chopped
1/3 white onion, finely chopped
1 clove garlic, minced

3 or 4 fresh sprigs of cilantro, remove stems and chopped
1 serrano chili, finely chopped
salt, pepper and fresh lime juice - to taste

> Blend all the ingredients together and let flavors develop for 1/2 hour before serving.

Eggs Benedict

4 English Muffins
8 small slices of ham
8 eggs
cayenne pepper
Pam
1 teaspoon vinegar

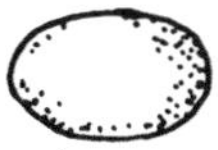

>Split English muffins and toast. Warm ham.
>Spray a flat bottomed pan with Pam. Fill half full with water and bring to a simmer on stove top. Add a teaspoon of vinegar to the water, this will help congeal the eggs. Break the eggs into a cup, not into the pan. Swirl the water around, then gently place the eggs to be poached, into the pan. Judge doneness by tapping the eggs lightly with the edge of a spoon.
>Layer a slice of ham, a poached egg and hollandaise sauce on top of each muffin half. Sprinkle with cayenne before serving.
Serves 4.

Hollandaise Sauce

1 cube (1/4 lb.) of butter, cut into thirds
3 egg yolks

The grade on egg cartons indicates freshness not size. Grade AA eggs are fresh fancy; Grade A eggs are good in appearance and flavor and can be used for most dishes; Grade B eggs should be used only for general cooking and baking.

The shell of the egg is a result of pigment, the yolk color that of feed. A fresh farm egg, produced by chickens who are well fed, will have a deep orange-yellow colored yolk.

Low heat is essential in cooking any mixture enriched with egg yolks. If your sauce separates, it is because it is too hot. You can rescue it by whisking in 1-2 Tablespoons of cream, or another egg yolk.

-Susan

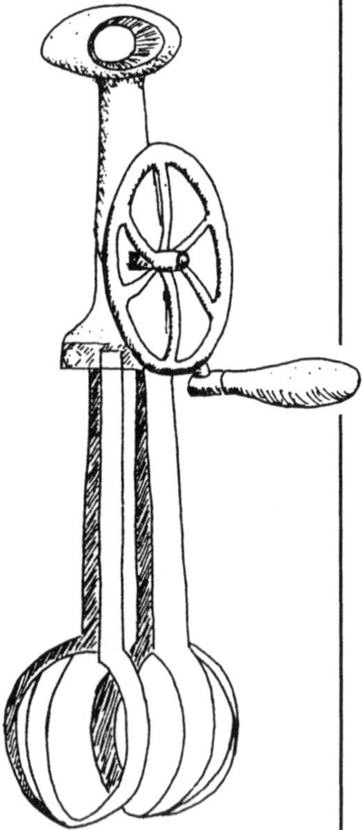

1 Tablespoon fresh squeezed lemon juice

>In the top of a double boiler, melt the first 1/3 of the butter cube. Whisk. Add second 1/3 and melt, whisk. Add last 1/3 to melt and whisk. Whisk in yolks and lemon juice.

Ian's Cheese Eggs

Ian is the youngest of our children. He has now passed the Boy Scout / live at home era. He became an Eagle Scout, Canadian Rowing Champion and has gone to the U.S. Naval Academy, but still cooks his Cheese Eggs when he comes home. Here is his recipe for cheese eggs. This dish is a favorite among teenagers, but not recommended for those on low cholesterol diets.

4 eggs
4 Tablespoons milk
2 Tablespoons butter
handful grated cheddar chesse

>Beat eggs with milk.
>Melt butter in non-stick pan.
>Add eggs, scrambling over low heat, stirring constantly.
>When partially cooked, add the cheese and finish cooking.

Serves 2.

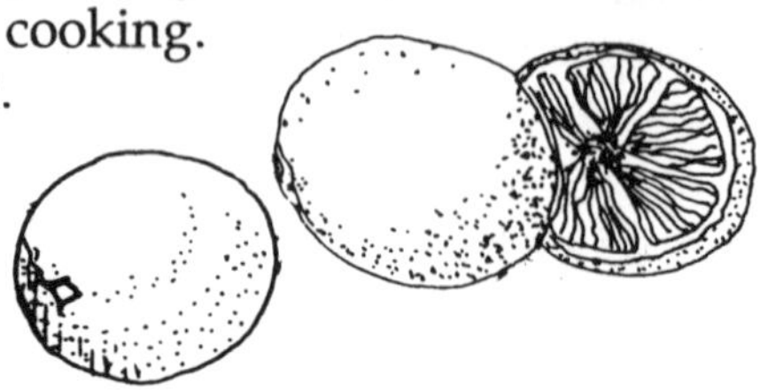

Fresh Mushroom Omelet

Omelets are fun to make. They make a wonderful breakfast or a tasty dinner. With a basic omelet recipe you can experiment, adding new fillings as your imagination allows.

---

10 eggs
3 Tablespoons water
1 pound mushrooms, sliced
1 Tablespoon snipped chives or 2 scallions, chopped
2 Tablespoons butter
1 Tablespoon fresh rosemary or 1 teaspoon dried
1/2 pound grated swiss or cheddar cheese

>Beat eggs in a blender with water. Do not overblend.
>Melt butter in a large frying pan and sauté mushrooms with chives and rosemary until the mushrooms begin to give off their liquor. Keep warm as you prepare omelet.
>Melt 1/2 teaspoon butter in an 8 inch frying pan (non-stick is best). Heat butter until bubbly, then add enough eggs to cover bottom of pan about 1/4 inch thick.
>Push eggs with spatula to center as you tilt pan, enabling uncooked eggs to flow over the set eggs. When almost done put a line of mushroom mixture down the center of omelet then add a handful of grated cheese.
>Fold the right then the left side over filling. Serve hot.

Makes 4 omelets.

Turtleback Farm Inn - Summer Breakfast on the Deck

Mixed fresh fruits served with Banana Cream or Cinnamon Cream
Turtleback Farm Inn Granola served with yogurt and golden raisins
Soufflé Roll with smoked Salmon or Mushroom/Spinach Filling
Angel Biscuits served with butter and jam.

Suggested Omelets:
chicken & tomato
sweet peppers & onion
sautéed potatoes & ham
asparagus & shallots
spinach & bacon
crab & asparagus
fruits in fruit sauce
cream cheese & jam

Quiche suggestions:
sautéed mushrooms
smoked salmon
flaked crabmeat
red & green peppers
broccoli
shrimp
spinach & bacon
asparagus & chicken

Creativity is allowing yourself to make mistakes. Art is knowing which ones to keep.
-Scott Adams

Quiche

Many cooks today buy frozen prepared shells for quiches and pies. Although the shells will work, I find them inferior to a homemade crust because they often break and can become soggy while cooking. Some cooks feel pie crust is too difficult and are hesitant to try. But, if you know a few simple tricks, you can make a flaky crust every time. And if you want, you can make several and freeze them for convenience.

Crust Recipe

3 cups flour
1 cup crisco
pinch salt
4 Tablespoons cold water

>Preheat oven to 350°.
>Cut the crisco into the flour using a food processor.
>Add water and salt.
>After processing flour etc., remove dough, pat into round, wrap in saran and chill before rolling.
>Roll the dough out carefully on a floured surface. The less you handle the dough the better. Overhandled dough has been stretched and will pull back when baked.
>Place dough into pie pan and flute the edges. Prick all over with a fork, especially the sides of the shell. This releases steam so the crust will not crack.
>To prevent the crust from becoming soggy, bake blind. First place a piece of wax paper along the bottom of the crust. Then cover with a handful of dried beans. This weights the crust down. Then bake for 15 minutes, unfilled. Allow to cool.

Basic quiche recipe

1 1/2 cups half & half
4 eggs, beat slightly
1 Tablespoon dijon mustard, this is a maximum, use less if preferred
pinch nutmeg
2 cups grated raw milk cheddar
1 cup filling of your choice

>Preheat oven to 415°.
>Beat half and half, eggs, mustard and nutmeg together.
>Line the bottom of the crust with your filling choice. My family prefers Quiche Lorraine, which is made with chopped ham. Other possibilities are listed in the margin. Cover your filling with cheese. Then pour liquid mixture over top.
>Bake for 10 minutes, then reduce oven temperature to 375°. Cook for 40 minutes. Check for overbrowning. If the quiche browns too much, cover the top with aluminum foil.
>Let cool for 10 minutes before cutting. This allows the quiche to set so it cuts clean.

Applying baking soda to grease splatters and other foods that have dried on the stove will help remove them. Just sprinkle on a little dry soda, then rub with a damp cloth. Rinse with water and wipe dry.

Soufflé Roll
My Mother's Recipe

The filling for the soufflé roll works great in an omelet.

4 Tablespoons butter
1/2 cup flour
1 teaspoon salt
pinch pepper
2 cups milk

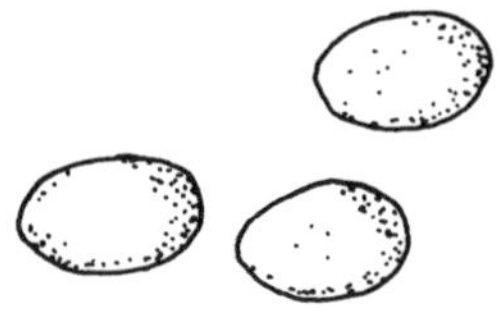

5 egg yolks
5 egg whites

Filling:

---

1 bunch spinach, cleaned, stemmed, and chopped, or 10 ounces frozen chopped spinach
1/2 pound mushrooms
2 Tablespoons butter
8 ounces cream cheese
pinch salt
pinch pepper

>Preheat oven to 400°. Have all ingredients ready as filling will be made while soufflé is baking.

>Melt 4 Tablespoons of butter in a saucepan. Blend in flour, salt and pepper.

>Whisk in milk, bringing the mixture to a boil. Stir constantly until thickened.

>Cool. Add the egg yolks, one by one, and beat.

>Beat the egg whites until stiff. Fold them into the cooled sauce.

>Line a jelly roll pan with waxed paper, then butter and flour it. Pour in the soufflé mixture, spreading lightly to form an even layer.

>Bake for 30 minutes or until nicely browned.

>Turn immediately onto a towel.

>While soufflé is baking, sauté spinach and mushrooms in 2 Tablespoons of butter until tender.

>Add the cream cheese and mix well. Season to taste.

>Spread the warm filling evenly over the warm soufflé and roll up jelly roll style with the help of a towel.

>Serve immediately.

This can be prepared ahead and stored overnight in the refrigerator. Warm thoroughly in the oven or microwave before serving.

-Susan

Northwest Eggs

If you do not have fresh dill, sprinkle some dried dill weed on the sour cream.

5 eggs
1 1/2 cups milk
1 teaspoon Dijon mustard
1 teaspoon lemon juice
4 ounces cream cheese
2 Tablespoons sour cream
1/2 teaspoon dill weed
2 teaspoons capers
8 ounces smoked salmon

> Preheat oven to 375°.
> Combine all the ingredients except the capers and the salmon in a blender. Blend until mixed. Add the capers and salmon and blend for a moment. Be careful not to purée the salmon.
> Pour into a buttered 10 inch pyrex dish and bake at 375° for about 40 minutes or until puffed and lightly browned.
> Remove from oven and let cool briefly to set. Cut into eight slices. Garnish each slice with a dollop of sour cream, a few capers and a sprig of fresh dill.
> Serve with muffins or biscuits.
Serves 8.

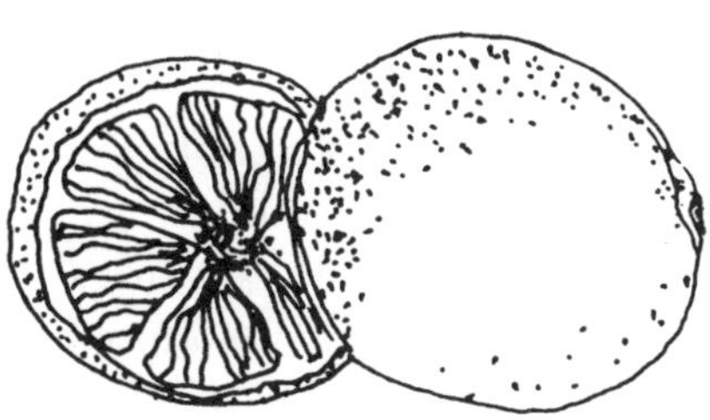

Vinegar is a great solution to use on lime deposits on coffeemakers, humidifiers, or tea kettles. Just soak with equal parts water.

Egg Tips
A fresh egg will hold together better when poaching. Older ones tend to separate and are not as flavorful. Never leave eggs, raw or cooked, out of the refrigerator for more than two hours. Refrigerate eggs in the carton, they are probably more sanitary than your refrigerator shelf. Also eggs should not be stored uncovered as they absorb odors and lose moisture.

What wisdom can you find that is greater than kindness?
- Jean-Jacques Rousseau

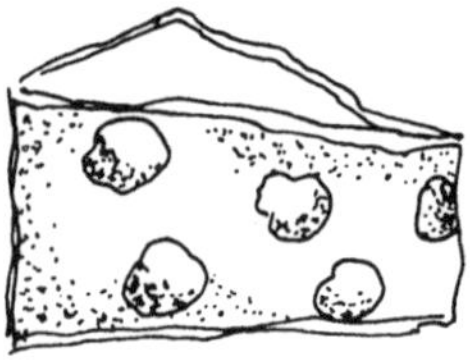

When washing easily broken items, place a dish towel in the sink to help prevent breakage.

Picture-Perfect Breakfast Pizza

4 cups all-purpose flour
1/2 cup cold butter, cut into bits
1 Tablespoon baking powder
pinch of salt
1 cup light cream or half and half
1 each; yellow, red and green bell peppers, thinly sliced
1 medium onion, thinly sliced
1 cup diced ham
1 1/2 Tablespoons butter
6 medium eggs
2 cups shredded cheese (raw milk cheddar or any medium to sharp cheese)

> Preheat oven to 425°.
> In the work bowl of a food processor (using a steel blade), blend the dough's dry ingredients with the butter until the mixture resembles coarse meal.
> Add the cream through the feed tube and blend briefly until the dough begins to gather into a ball.
> Remove the dough and pat into a round on a floured board. Let rest for a few minutes.
> Sauté the peppers, onion, ham and butter in a skillet until the peppers and the onion become soft. Set aside.
> Divide the dough into 6 equal pieces. Roll each piece on the floured board into a 8 inch round. Pinch the outside edge into a 1/2 inch rim around each circle. The diameter of each round will now be approximately 5 inches.
> Transfer each round to a buttered cookie

sheet. Top each round with the pepper mixture, leaving a well in the center. Bake 10 minutes, then break egg into the center and top with about 1/3 cup shredded cheese and return to oven.
> Bake until eggs are set. Serve immediately.
Serves 6.

There must be as many fritatta recipes as there are cooks preparing them. Many combinations of fresh vegetables work very well. Experiment until you find the combination you like the best.

- Susan

Breakfast Fritatta

2 red potatoes, cooked until just tender
3 Tablespoons olive oil
1 zucchini, thinly sliced
1 red bell pepper, cored, seeded and sliced into thin strips
1/2 pound mushrooms, thinly sliced
2 scallions, chopped tops included
1 medium onion, thinly sliced
2 cloves, minced
1 bunch spinach, washed, stemmed and roughly chopped
1 fresh tomato, sliced
10 eggs
1/2 cup grated parmesan cheese
1 cup raw milk cheddar, grated

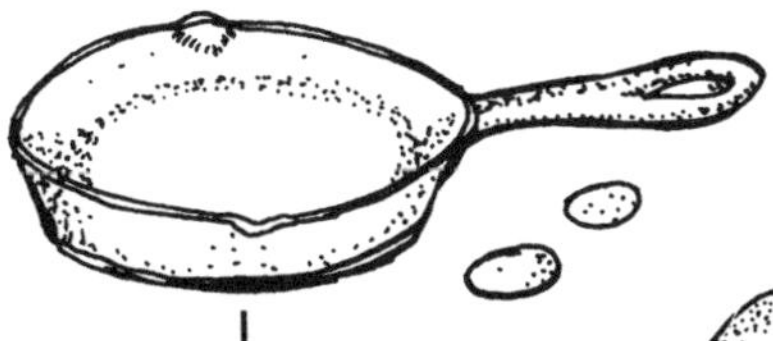

> In a 10 inch skillet (I usually use a cast iron one because it can readily go into the oven) sauté onion and garlic in 1 Tablespoon olive oil until tender. Set aside in a bowl.
> In the same skillet, adding more olive oil if needed, sauté mushrooms, scallions, red pepper and zucchini until also tender. Add the spinach and stir until it is wilted. Add these to the onion/garlic mixture.

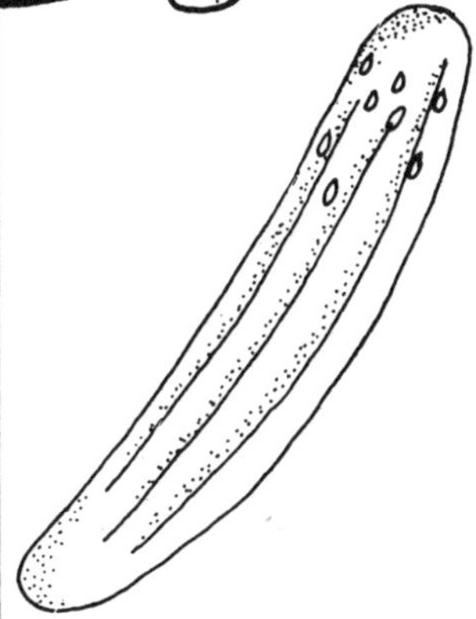

Chèvre has become one of my favorite cheeses. There are many kinds that appeal to a wide range of palates. Most are made from all goats' milk but some are mixed with cows' milk and have a creamier consistency. Chèvre has a tangy taste and is widely available. It is wonderful crumbled on a salad and goes well with potatoes, fruit, and substitutes well for ricotta and feta in baked recipes.

- Susan

Life is a great big canvas, and you should throw all the paint on it you can.
. . . Danny Kaye

> Slice the potatoes thinly and place them on the bottom of the skillet, covering the surface and a bit up the sides.
> Fill the pan with the cooked vegetables, top with the grated cheddar cheese and finally the sliced tomatoes.
> Blend the eggs with salt and pepper and pour over the ingredients.
> Cook on top of the stove at medium heat without stirring until the eggs begin to set, about 8 minutes.
> Sprinkle with parmesan cheese and place in a 400° oven until the cheese is bubbling and the eggs set. This takes about 4-6 more minutes.
> Remove from oven and cool a few minutes before slicing. Serve warm.

Serves 6-8.

Blintz Soufflé

1/4 pound butter, softened
6 eggs
1 cup sour cream
1/2 cup orange juice
1 cup flour
2 teaspoons baking powder
3 Tablespoons sugar
8 ounces cream cheese, cut up
1 pound cottage cheese
2 egg yolks
1 teaspoon vanilla

> Preheat oven to 350°. Butter a 13 inch x 9 inch baking pan.
> Blend together the first six ingredients and 2 Tablespoons of the sugar. Pour 1/2 the mixture into the bottom of the prepared dish. Set the remaining 1/2 mixture aside.
> Combine the remaining ingredients in a food processor, processing until smooth.
> Drop by spoonfuls over the batter in the bottom of the pan. With a knife, spread the top layer as smoothly as possible over the bottom layer.
> Pour remaining batter into the pan. (Unbaked soufflé may be covered and refrigerated overnight until ready to use.)
> Bring soufflé to room temperature. Bake uncovered 50 - 60 minutes or until soft and golden.
> Serve immediately with a topping of fruit sauce and a dollop of sour cream. Fresh fruit on the top is also tasty.

Serves 8.

Rubbing salad oil on the grater before you use it makes for easier cleanup when you are finished.

This may be prepared a day ahead and baked before serving.
- Susan

Washington's Best Loved Fruits

Apples - All strains of apples listed store well except Gravensteins, which should be eaten within two weeks of picking. Apples store best in a cool, dry, dark place such as a cellar. Below are some Washington state apples, their seasons and their uses.

Gravenstein - large, light green and red strains sweet and juicy	early Sept.	cooking & eating
Summerred - dark red with speckles tart, firm, fine texture	Aug. thru Sept.	cooking
Mutsu - large yellow-green juicy, crisp, spicy tart	Oct. - Nov.	excellent cooking
Spartan - red with pure white flesh mild, juicy and crisp	Oct.	eating
Jonagold - large yellow with red stripes crisp and juicy	Oct.	eating
Liberty - red stripes on yellow background crisp, juicy and sweet	late Sept.	eating
Melrose - large, quiet red sugary sweet, slightly tart	Oct. - Nov.	excellent eating & cooking

Pears Pears are ripe if the stem end gives a little when pressed. Select firm, slightly underripe pears and let them ripen in a bowl or paper bag. Slightly underripe pears are best for cooking. Pears become overripe quickly, so use soon after ripening.

Bosc - long necked, russet hue over golden skin tart flavor, buttery texture	Oct. - May	cooking
Bartlett - large and bell shaped sweet, musky flavor	Aug. - Nov.	eating
Anjou - russet colored, egg shaped sweet, wine-like flavor	Oct. - May	cooking & eating
Comice - round and green sweet and juicy	Oct. - May	eating

Berries - Berries are very versatile and can be used for garnish, sorbets, ice creams, parfaits, tarts, cobblers, pies, muffins, jams, sauces, wines, vinegars, chutneys, or served fresh. Unless frozen, berries should be refrigerated and eaten within a week. The favorite berries grown in Washington and their seasons are blackberries (July - Sept.), strawberries (April - July) and blueberries (June - Aug.).

The Pig War

Orcas Island is one island in a chain of 273 (at high tide) known as the San Juans. These islands are located in the Strait of Juan de Fuca and are a part of Washington State.

Originally, the islands were claimed by both Great Britain and the United States. Both sides agreed that the 49th parallel up to Point Roberts at the sea was the boundary between United States and British territories. At Point Roberts, they disagreed which of two channels the line should follow. The British proposed that the line follow Rosario Channel, which would have made the San Juans a part of British Columbia. The Americans wanted the line to run through De Haro Straits, making the islands a United States territory.

Both countries kept troops posted in the area, creating a conflict of authority. It was commonplace for those accused of crimes by one side to claim protection from the other. For this reason, the islands soon became a gathering place for outlaws.

Many settlers in the San Juans were former employees of the Canadian owned Hudson Bay Company. The company conducted fur trade in the area, employing men from American territories and Canada. Company policy encouraged employees to take Indian wives, both to obtain control of trade and to insure against uprisings. These Native American women were purchased for prices ranging from $20.00 to $50.00 according to looks and social standing in the tribe. Men who married these women were called "squaw men."

In 1859, an American settler named Lyman Cutler became frustrated by a Hudson Bay Company pig that had broken down his fences and rooted his garden. He killed the pig with his rifle, then felt remorseful and went to the company to make restitution. He asked the clerk what the pig was worth and was told it was a prize breeder worth $100.00. With the best wives going for $50.00 and whole farms for $200.00, Cutler thought the price was too high and refused to pay.

Both sides claimed injury in the incident. The United States sent in troops to settle the matter and the British countered with war ships. Hotheads on both sides demanded war, but fortunately cooler heads prevailed and the issue was settled through mediation. Because the only casualty of the confrontation was the pig, the incident came to be known as "The Pig War."

Several years passed before the boundary matter was settled, however. In 1872, the German Kaiser was called upon to decide the boundaries and settled in favor of the United States. A reasonable time was given to the claimants of land in the area to settle their affairs.

As a side note, the Hudson Bay Company's interest in the San Juan Islands was primarily in mink, which were trapped to extinction in the area.

Against the protests of local Native Americans, white settlers moved into the area in large numbers and began clear cutting and establishing farms. A society was formed to encourage white settlers moving into the area and another organization's purpose was to discourage the Chinese from moving to the San Juans. Within a few years, the Indians no longer lived on Orcas Island. It was a farming community and one of the top apple producing areas in the state.

Turtleback Farm is a working farm. The Fletchers do not plant a crop each year to take to market, but they do tend their orchards, raise chickens and sheep and harvest hay. They also cultivate gardens. Many wildflowers graced the farm before the Fletchers came, but the flower gardens they have established since their arrival are breath-taking.

Being raised in the city, I had little exposure to flower gardens as a child. I think that Michael was lucky; he grew up on a farm. I have always thought that growing up in the country, with clean air and water, wide open spaces and a horse or two, was idyllic. Michael agrees it was wonderful, but points out that a farm is a lot of work.

I found that out when I planted my first garden at the age of twenty-two. It consisted of a few fruits and vegetables because I considered myself a practical person; flowers to me were not practical. Fully into the experience I canned fruit, made pickles and jams and froze vegetables. The garden gave me a huge return for my work, but it was years later before I understood the practical side of beauty.

Recent studies by Japanese researchers have shown that flower scents delivered throughout large building via air-conditioning systems have the power to soothe the weary, lessen mental fatigue and induce calmness. Perhaps this is our unconscious motivation for giving one another flowers and perfumes. Far back into recorded history people have given flowers as symbols of victory, prosperity and admiration. Although we are not sure what our distant ancestors knew about plants that brought about this gift of flowers, we are coming to understand more fully the gifts that plants give us.

Plants have always been known for their food value. Fruits,

nuts, leaves, roots and flowers are all common to the human diet. For centuries, among various cultures including those of western civilization, flowers and herbs were a staple. Even today, cooks include flowers in their menus without realizing it. Broccoli, cauliflower and artichokes are flower buds, as well as common foods. Marigolds, borage, gladiolus, lilacs and nasturtiums are not often used today, but for centuries these flowers were as common to the diet as broccoli is now.

Chrysanthemums were a part of Confucius' diet. Greek historians tell us that the Persians ate nasturtiums. The Romans and the Greeks celebrated enormous banquets that included rose petals and violets. When cooking became fashionable in seventeenth century Europe, obtaining, preparing and preserving food was not a simple matter. Fresh fruits, meats and vegetables were not readily available. So, flowers, spices and herbs were heavily relied upon.

These ingredients were known to have medicinal properties, as well as food value. Earlier cultures knew that food is more than just something to satisfy the appetite. The word restaurant comes from the same Old French word that gives us the words restore and restoration because early inns served hearty broths that were known for their healing properties. Even today, some remote cultures have practicing herbalists, and scientists are discovering anew the healing properties of food.

Michael and I had our first experience with flower cuisine in a restaurant. When our plates were brought to the table, they were beautifully garnished with nasturtiums. After we expressed hesitancy about the wisdom of this, the server assured us that they were safe to eat. She also told us that the flowers are high in vitamin C and contain a herbal type penicillin that helps ward off infection.

Since that meal we have seen flowers in many kitchens and I have planted a flower garden. Flowers contribute to the beauty of a salad, add an unusual taste to soups, float gracefully in a glass of wine, and garnish a cake beautifully.

In recommending flowers for the kitchen, we suggest that

you grow your own. Many flowers bought in stores today contain chemicals which are not safe to eat. If you do buy flowers from a local florist or nursery, be certain they are organically grown. Before using, always wash the flowers gently to rinse off any dirt or residues.

When we first tried flower cuisine, we were a little nervous because we know powerful medicines come from flowers. Poppies are the source of a number of pain killers and foxglove gives us heart medication. Our ancestors were not ignorant because they used botanical medicines, we still do. Unfortunately, many people are not as familiar with nature as their grandparents.

But we learned there are many ways of finding out which plants are safe to eat and which ones are too powerful for our systems. We found books at the library which helped us identify the flowers which are safe in a given area. *Field Guide to Edible Wild Plants* by Angier is an authoritative guide to plants and their habitats in the United States and Canada. *The Edible Wild* by Berglund and Bolsby and *Stalking the Wild Asparagus* by Gibbons may also be helpful. If you are interested in finding out about plants in your area, the county extension agent may shed some light on the subject. We found our local nursery quite knowledgeable. Botany departments of local schools may also provide information. On Orcas Island, two local residents give annual walks through the woods to identify which plants are edible. Perhaps a botanist in your area gives such a tour. Animals also provide us clues to what is edible, but because their systems are different, they are not a foolproof barometer.

On Orcas Island, because there are no natural predators, the local deer feel safe eating out of your hand. They also help themselves to residents' flowers. Gardeners grumble somewhat good naturedly about it and put high fences around their prize vegetable and flower gardens. The deer, however, have the good sense to know which flowers are unhealthy. On Orcas, these are the ones growing undisturbed along the roadway.

In the next two recipes you can substitute half & half or yogurt for the sour cream to reduce calories and cholesterol.
-Susan

He that is of a merry heart has a continual feast.
. . .Proverbs 15:15

Soups

From time to time, I have fixed picnic baskets for honeymoon couples. These soups are great thermos fillers. They are especially good with sourdough bread. If you bring along fruit and cookies, you have a complete meal.

Summer Beet Soup

3 medium to large beets, unpeeled and scrubbed
4 cups buttermilk
2 cups sour cream
1/2 cup lemon juice
1/2 cup finely minced scallions, tops and all
2 large cloves garlic, minced
salt
pepper
1 lime, thinly sliced for garnishment

>Cook beets in boiling water until very tender when pierced with a fork, about 45 minutes. Drain and allow to cool until they can be handled.
>Slip off the skin and cube the beets finely. Set aside 3/4 cup for garnish.
>Using a blender or a food processor, purée the beets in the buttermilk until smooth.
>In a large bowl, mix the beet purée with the sour cream, lemon juice, scallions and minced garlic. Season to taste. Whisk until completely blended.
>Add the reserved beets and chill overnight.
>Before serving taste for seasoning, adding more lemon juice if needed. Garnish with a lime slice.

Cucumber Soup

2 cucumbers
1/4 cup chopped parsley
1 leek, white part only
1 pint sour cream
1 teaspoon salt
2 Tablespoons lemon juice
4 cups buttermilk
2 Tablespoons fresh dill, for garnishment

>Peel, seed and chop cucumbers except for six thin slices to be used for garnish. Put half the cucumber in a blender with half of the leeks and parsley and 2 cups buttermilk. Blend until smooth. Remove from the blender.

>Repeat with the remaining cucumber, parsley, leeks, buttermilk and salt.

>Blend the two mixtures together. Whisk in sour cream and lemon juice.

>Chill until serving time. Add the dill and cucumber as you serve.

Suggested Garnishes:
almond slivers
diced apples with skins
avocado slices
thinly sliced carrots
cauliflower buds
chopped celery
grated cheese
sour cream
chopped fresh herbs
sliced olives
orange peel
thinly sliced radishes
small cooked shrimp, deveined and shelled
diced tomato
chopped scallions

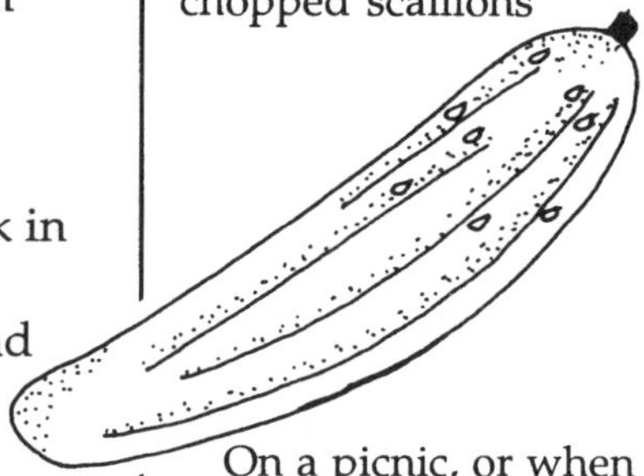

On a picnic, or when brown bagging to work, plan on eating light. A touch of something unique will break up the lunchtime doldrums and leave you feeling satisfied better than a large amount of food. Then you are not faced with leftovers or that sleepy, too full feeling at mid-day.

Gazpacho

1 clove garlic
2 teaspoons salt
1/2 cup chopped mushrooms
3 Tablespoons olive oil
1 cup scallions, finely chopped, tops and all
2 cups tomatoes, finely chopped
1 cup red or green peppers, finely chopped
1 cup cucumber, peeled and finely chopped
2 teaspoons chives
1 Tablespoon chopped parsley

How to dry flowers
Pick blossoms just before they open and place in cool water overnight.

Pour an even one inch layer of fine dry sand into a large flat box. Gently dry the flowers with a towel and remove any leaves. Place flowers on the sand without allowing plants to touch each other. Cover completely with sand.

Cover and set box in a warm dry place and allow flowers to dry completely. To store flowers, hang them upside down or stand them upright in a vase.

1 teaspoon finely ground pepper
1/4-1/2 teaspoon tabasco
1 teaspoon Worcestershire sauce
1/2 cup tarragon wine vinegar
3 cups tomato juice
lemon juice to taste

>Crush garlic in the salt.
>Sauté mushrooms in olive oil until just lightly browned.
>Combine all the ingredients together. If you use a food processor, be certain to chop the ingredients, not purée them. Do not use a blender. Cover and chill overnight. Use a glass or stainless steel bowl for storage, not an aluminum one.
>When ready to serve, correct the seasoning, adding lemon juice and seasoning to taste.

Mushroom Soup

This soup resembles a cream soup as it is quite thick. The advantage is that it is the real thing - mushroom soup without the cream or flour thickeners often found in cream soups.

1 1/2 pounds mushrooms, chopped
2 Tablespoons butter
3 shallots, minced fine
6 cups chicken broth
1 teaspoon lemon juice
1/2 teaspoon salt

>Heat butter in a large saucepan. Sauté shallots and mushrooms over medium

heat for 7-10 minutes or until they are soft and have given up their liquor.
>Add chicken broth. Cook slowly for 30 minutes.
>Purée in blender and season with salt and lemon juice to taste.
>Serve hot.

Cauliflower Soup

In the past, many recipes for cream soups called for the addition of heavy cream or half and half. I have had excellent results using more vegetables and eliminating the high calorie and high fat cream.

2 ribs celery, chopped, and a few tops too
1 medium onion, finely chopped
3 Tablespoons butter
1 large head cauliflower
4 cups chicken broth
2 cups milk

>In a large saucepan, sauté celery and onion in butter until lightly browned and soft.
>Cut cauliflower head into small pieces. Use all of the head, but not the leaves. Add to the pan with the onion.
>Cover with chicken broth and simmer until cauliflower is very soft.
>Purée in blender until smooth.
>Add milk and reheat. Season to taste with salt and pepper.
>Serve warm or cold with a grating of fresh nutmeg.

The cauliflower soup recipe can be used as the basis for almost any vegetable soup. Simply substitute broccoli, spinach, sorrel or pumpkin for the cauliflower. I would add a touch of additional flavoring for seasoning. Dill goes well in broccoli soup, a little lemon juice works well with spinach or sorrel and nutmeg is great in pumpkin soup. I like to make the pumpkin soup at Halloween with our leftover Jack-O-Lantern. This works well as long as you don't leave your pumpkin out too long or allow it to get too dirty.

-Susan

Presentation is important. Whether you are serving a picnic, a formal dinner or a party brunch, keep in mind that your guests, and you, will see and smell the dish before you taste it. Colorful dishes make an important first impression on the palate.

-Susan

People often overlook herbs as a landscaping plant. Yet, many herbs have longevity, looks, and low maintenance requirements, as well as being edible. Think about rosemary, thyme, lavender, sage, sweet basil, mint or any number of herbs not only as garden plants, but as possible front yard plants too. Be careful where you plant herbs. Some can become invasive if left unattended.

Not Quite So Rich Potato Soup

This soup is our version of Vichyssoise – a cold cream enriched potato soup. In the French version, the recipe calls for 1/2 & 1/2 and a finish of heavy cream. Here we use more potatoes and stock. If you prefer, you can always make it richer with the addition of 1/2 & 1/2 and/or heavy cream. It can be served hot or cold.

---

6 large leeks, washed carefully and the white part thinly sliced
1/2 lb. white mushrooms, thinly sliced
4 Tbs. butter
5 cups chicken stock
5 medium potatoes, peeled and diced
1 cup whole milk
Salt and freshly ground pepper to taste
A dollop of sour cream and chopped fresh chives for garnish

> In a large saucepan, melt butter and sauté sliced leeks and mushrooms for about 5 minutes stirring so as not to scorch them. Add chicken stock, salt and pepper and bring to a boil. Add potatoes and simmer until the potatoes are thoroughly cooked.

> Cool and put with milk into blender. (Be certain not to try to blend the ingredients when hot or you will be cleaning up the kitchen ceiling.) Blend until smooth. Garnish and serve either hot or cold.

> If serving hot, re-heat using a double boiler or a "flame tamer". Do not allow soup to boil.

Creatures of the Sea Soup

1 lb. firm fresh fish such a snapper, salmon or cod cut into chunks
1/2 lb. mussels or clams, well scrubbed
1/2 lb. scallops or shrimp
1 cup pealed and diced boiled potatoes
1/3 cup minced celery
1/3 cup minced onion
1/3 cup sliced mushrooms
1 bottle clam juice
2 cups fish stock
2 Tbs. olive oil
2 Tbs. butter (can be all olive oil)
1/4 cup sherry or white wine
salt and pepper to taste

> In a large, heavy saucepan, heat oil and butter and sauté celery, onion and mushrooms until limp being careful not to scorch.

> Add stock and clam juice and the remaining ingredients.

> Cook gently until shells open and fish is done.

> Serve hot with a tossed green salad and plenty of Sourdough bread.

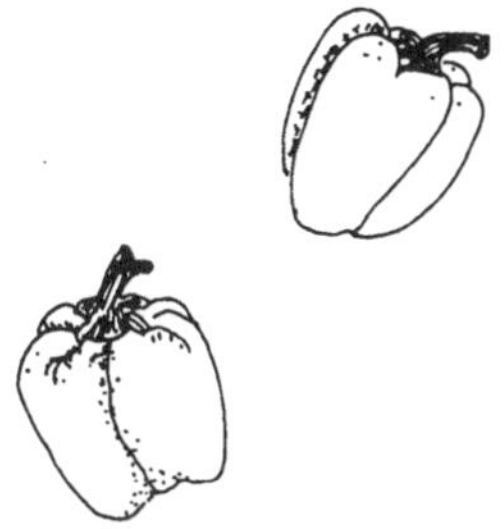

I make a lot of soups from stuff I find in the refrigerator. I chop up an onion and some celery tops and ribs, add a clove or two of crushed garlic, then soften these in a big pot with some olive oil, being careful not to scorch the ingredients. Lastly I add the main ingredient and water and stock to cover. When thoroughly cooked, I purée this in the blender without adding milk or cream. Add salt and pepper to taste and you will have a creamy and rich soup without a lot of calories

-Susan

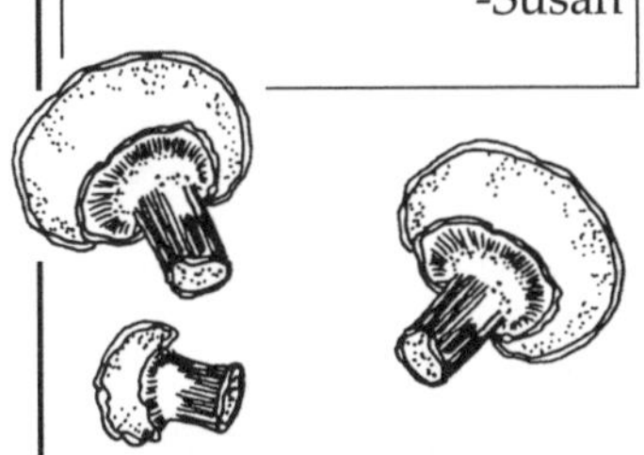

Recipe for candied flowers

1 1/2 cups sugar
1/2 cup water
fresh edible petals
tweezers
food coloring (optional)

Make a syrup of 1 cup sugar and 1/2 cup water. Boil until it spins a thread. Cool to room temperature. Gently wash and dry petals (whole flowers may also be used). Using the tweezers, dip the petals into the syrup. Shake off any excess and dip into the remaining sugar. Place on waxed paper to dry.

You may also color the sugar the same color as the flower, using food coloring. Allow the mixture to dry thoroughly, stirring occasionally, before use.

Best Flowers for Candy

Rose petals
Gardenia Petals
Mint Leaves
Borage
Violets
Lilacs
Orange Blossoms
Lemon or Lime Blossoms

Armenian Cracker Bread Sandwich Rolls

This is a lunch recipe that makes a good snack or hors d' oeuvres. Vegetarians will find it works well with eggs substituted for the beef.

a large round Armenian cracker bread
1 - 3 ounce package of cream cheese, beaten until light and fluffy
1 Tablespoon prepared horseradish
1/4 teaspoon pepper
1 Tablespoon milk
1/2 pound thinly sliced roast beef
1 cup alfalfa sprouts
2 medium tomatoes, very thinly sliced

>Soften cracker bread by holding it under a light spray of cold water for about 10 seconds on each side, or until well moistened, but not soggy. Place between clean, damp towels and let stand until soft and pliable. If there are still some crisp spots, sprinkle additional water over them.

>Mix cream cheese, horseradish and pepper. Stir in milk so cheese will spread easily. Spread the round of cracker bread with cheese mixture. Top with roast beef, sprouts and tomato slices.

>Roll up tightly and wrap in damp towel. Slice just prior to serving.

Flank Steak Pita Pockets

1 flank steak
1 cup olive oil
1/2 cup soy sauce
1 onion, chopped
2 garlic cloves
3 Tablespoons vinegar
2 Tablespoons honey
pita bread pockets
tomato slices
alfalfa sprouts

>Mix all of the ingredients except steak in a blender.
>Marinate steak in sauce at least 3 hours or overnight.
>Grill on hot grill 5-6 minutes per side.
>Slice thinly on the diagonal. Serve in pita bread pockets with mustard, tomato slices and sprouts.

Makes 4 well-filled pockets.

Lamb Patties in Pita Pockets

1 pound ground lamb
1 clove garlic, minced
1/2 small onion, finely chopped
1/2 teaspoon cinnamon
1 teaspoon chopped parsley
1/2 teaspoon dried mint
1/2 teaspoon cumin
salt and pepper to taste
pocket bread

At home we serve flank steak marinated and barbecued. This recipe works great with chicken too.
-Susan

A marinade is a liquid that seasons and tenderizes meats. It was originally used by sailors to preserve fish. The word comes from the French, meaning "to pickle in brine." Before marinades were used, salt alone was used as a preservative. A basic marinade consists of two parts oil, one part vinegar, one onion or garlic and seasonings, herbs and spices to taste.

> Mix the ground lamb with the other ingredients. Shape into patties and grill on the barbecue.
> Serve with sliced and heated pocket bread as a container, accompanied by spiced yogurt, shredded lettuce and sliced tomatoes.

When making sandwiches, always keep your mind open to interesting containers. Just switching to a different bread or a roll can often make the difference between an interesting sandwich and a boring one.

Spiced Yogurt

1 cup yogurt
1 teaspoon cumin
1 teaspoon mint

> Combine and let the flavors blend. Serve chilled with grilled lamb.

When wrapping foods to be eaten later, keep in mind that aluminum foil will stay in place better than plastic wrap, is recyclable and has better insulating properties. You also might want to label foods for easy identification.

Savory Crisps

This can be used instead of crackers with any cheese or spread. Served with fruits and cheese, it is the simplest, most basic of lunch menus. If you sprinkle these with parmesan cheese before baking, they are a wonderful accompaniment for a bowl of soup. At Turtleback, we serve the Smoked Salmon Appetizer on page 87 with these little crisps.

1 loaf whole grain bread
1/4 pound butter
1 teaspoon savory
1 teaspoon sweet basil
2 teaspoons finely minced chives

>Preheat oven to 350°.
>Remove crusts from bread. Cut bread in half on the diagonal.
>Blend butter and herbs and spread on one side of the bread.
>Bake butter side up for about 30 minutes.

Smoked Salmon Appetizer

Even though this dish is chilled, it is served at room temperature. This makes it a good buffet dish or something to serve when everyone is not eating at the same time. I also recommend this dish for a romantic picnic. It sets an elegant mood, especially if you take along fresh flowers, a white table-cloth and real wine glasses.

12 ounces smoked salmon
1/3 cup minced red onion
2 Tablespoons capers, drained
3 Tablespoons Vodka
1 Tablespoon fresh dill (or 1 1/2 teaspoons dried)
1/2 teaspoon ground black pepper, or to taste
1 Tablespoon fresh lemon juice
1/2 teaspoon minced lemon rind

>Bone the smoked salmon and mince.
>Place salmon in a bowl and stir in the remaining ingredients.
>Chill for at least one hour, but let sit at room temperature for about 15 minutes before serving. Serve with savory crisps.

Carnation Vinegar
Gently but thoroughly wash 2 Carnations. Hold the flower and pull the petals en masse from the stem. Clip off the heels. Place petals in a pint jar. Cover with a good cider vinegar and let the mixture stand for 10 days. Strain before use. This is especially good on fruit salads.

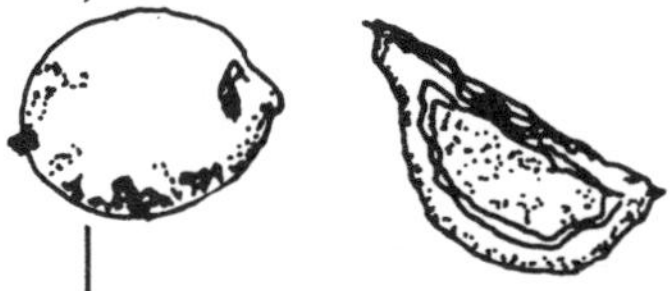

Pack the supplies you will need last at the bottom of your picnic basket and things you will need first on the top. This way your picnic can unpack in its natural sequence.

To renew old apple trees, use fresh made lime from the kiln. Slake it well with water and go over the tree thoroughly with a large stiff brush. The outer bark will fall off, insects and moss will be destroyed and a new, smooth healthy bark will form.

Holiday Green Sauce

I like to take this dip on a picnic with a basket of fresh vegetables and cookies for dessert. It is easy to prepare, makes a good potluck carry along or a wonderful hors d' oeuvres.

2 cups mayonnaise
1/3 cup minced parsley
1/3 cup minced scallions
1 cup minced spinach leaves (spines removed)
1/3 cup sour cream
2 Tablespoons fresh lemon juice
2 Tablespoons onion
dash Worcestershire

>Whirl everything in a blender or a food processor. Chill.
>Serve in hollowed out red cabbage on a bed of curly leafed lettuce in a festive basket. Surround with assorted raw vegetables; carrot sticks, bell pepper slices, cauliflower florets, zucchini spears, cherry tomatoes, mushrooms, radishes and/or celery sticks.

Chicken Pacifica

Because it can be served cold, this is a favorite picnic dish. It also makes a great appetizer.

2 packages chicken wing drummettes
1/2 cup brown sugar
1 cube butter

1 cup soy sauce
3/4 cup water
1 teaspoon dry mustard

>Mix all ingredients except chicken in a saucepan and heat until blended. Cool.
>Add chicken to cooled sauce. Marinate 2 or more hours, turning occasionally.
>Bake in sauce at 350° for 1 hour. Drain.
>Serve hot or cold.
Serves 12 as an appetizer.

Artichoke Frittata

Even though it is made with eggs, this dish serves well at room temperature.

---

12 ounces marinated artichoke bottoms or hearts
1 medium onion, chopped
2 cloves garlic, minced
4 eggs
1/2 cup fine, dry bread crumbs
1/2 teaspoon salt
1/4 teaspoon oregano
1/4 teaspoon pepper
1/8 teaspoon cayenne
2 cups shredded sharp cheddar cheese
2 Tablespoons minced parsley

>Preheat oven to 325°.
>Drain marinade from the artichokes into a skillet. Set the artichokes aside. Add onion and garlic to the skillet and sauté until onion is limp, about 5 minutes.
>In a bowl, beat eggs with a fork. Mix in

Will you teach your children what we have taught our children? That the earth is our mother? What befalls the earth, befalls all the sons of the earth.

This we know: The earth does not belong to man, man belongs to the earth... Man did not weave the web of life, he is merely a strand in it. Whatever he does to the web, he does to himself.

. . . Chief Seattle

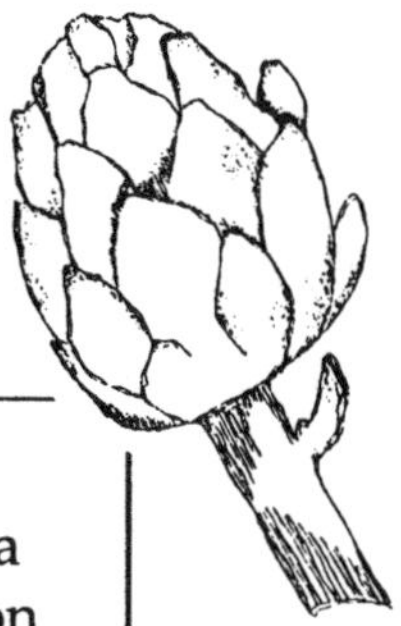

Distilled Vinegar, probably the most common household variety, is harsh and highly acidic, invaluable for pickling, but less useful for salads.

Cider Vinegar tastes unmistakably of its apple origins. Its flavor can overpower all but the strongest oils.

Rice Vinegars are light, pleasant and mild, good with delicate greens and quiet oils.

Balsamic Vinegar is made from grape must. A wonderful, red-brown, semisweet vinegar, it deserves a place on your shelf.

Herb Vinegars are very popular now. The only difficulty with them is that they predetermine the vinegar/herb combination in the night's salad.

Fruit Vinegars are actually revivals. Great for cooking fish and chicken.

crumbs, salt, pepper, cayenne and oregano.
>Stir in cheese, parsley, artichokes and the onion/garlic mixture.
>Turn into a buttered 9 inch x 13 inch baking dish. Bake at 325° for about 30 minutes or until set. Let cool in the pan.
>After cooled, cut into bite size squares.
Serves 12 as an appetizer.

Gourges - Little Cheese Puffs

These tasty little puffs are easy to prepare and serve as a great snack, appetizer, or as an accompaniment to a first course. They can be split and filled with your favorite mixture.

1 cup water
5 Tablespoons butter
1 teaspoon salt
1/2 teaspoon freshly ground black pepper
1/4 teaspoon freshly ground nutmeg
1 cup unbleached flour
1 cup grated Gruyère cheese
4 large eggs at room temperature
Egg wash - 1 large egg mixed with 1/2 Tablespoon water

> Preheat oven to 425°. Lightly grease a cookie sheet.
> In a medium saucepan, bring water, butter, salt, pepper, and nutmeg to a boil over medium high heat.
> As soon as the butter melts, reduce heat to low and add flour all at once. Cook over low heat, beating with wooden spoon until the mixture pulls away from the sides of the pan, about one minute.

> Remove pan from heat and add cheese, beating with the wooden spoon until the cheese is well blended.
> Add the four eggs, one at a time, beating each egg thoroughly into the batter. After the last egg has been incorporated, continue to beat until the mixture is smooth, shiny, and firm.
> Drop batter by small spoonfuls onto prepared cookie sheet, brushing tops with egg wash. Bake for 15 - 20 minutes or until the puffs have doubled in size and are golden.
> Remove from oven and serve hot, or cool and serve at room temperature.

Glazed Bratwurst

Pasta makes a great side dish for these sausages. Other types of sausages can be prepared this way as well.

1 1/2 pounds bratwurst
4 mushrooms, thinly sliced
3 Tablespoons butter
1 cup white wine
2 green onions, finely chopped
1 1/2 teaspoons Dijon mustard
1 1/2 Tablespoons chopped parsley

> Place sausages in a large skillet, cover with water and boil gently for about 10 minutes.
> Drain and melt 1 Tablespoon of the butter in the same pan. Add the mushrooms to the pan and cook with the sausages until they are lightly brown. When done, set

As a member of an escorted tour, you don't even have to know the Matterhorn isn't a tuba.
. . .Temple Fielding

The sausage is a cunning bird
With feathers long and wavy;
It swims about the frying pan
And makes its nest in gravy.
- Anonymous

Annuals are the jump starters of the garden. No other plant can produce such continuous color over a long period of time. Annuals are considered temporary plants, although some will reseed themselves from year to year. Below are some favorite annuals and their blooming seasons:

Spring - Fall
Allyssum
Begonia
Geranium
Impatiens
Petunias
Sweet William
Zinnias

Summer - Fall
Asters
Cosmos
Dahlias
Holly Hocks
Marigolds

Year Around in Mild Climates
Johnny Jump Ups
Pansies

aside and keep warm.

> Remove fat from the pan, but retain any crusty particles. Melt the remaining butter and heat until it begins to color. Add green onions and cook briefly.
> Add the wine, stirring constantly until the sauce is reduced a bit, then add the mustard and parsley.
> Pour the mixture over the sausages and serve.

Cabbage and Pea Salad with Pecans

Laurie Anderson owns and operates a wonderful inn with her husband, David Campiche. The Shelburne Inn is located on the coast in Seaview, Washington and Laurie and David serve many interesting and tasty treats. She shared this recipe with me a few years back and it is always a favorite. I recently made it for a fund raising dinner and the guests bought all the salad that was left. They wanted to buy the recipe too, but I said they had to wait for the new cookbook to come out.

2 - 10 ounce packages of frozen petit peas, thawed
2 cups cabbage, shredded
3 to 5 green onions, chopped including the tops
2 cans water chestnuts, chopped
2 cups pecans, lightly toasted and coarsely chopped
1/2 cup mayonnaise

1/2 cup sour cream
2 Tablespoons vinegar, red or white
1 teaspoon Dijon mustard, more if your taste prefers
1/2 to 1 teaspoon curry powder
salt and pepper to taste

> Combine peas, cabbage, onions, chestnuts and pecans in a large bowl.
> In a separate bowl, blend together mayonnaise, sour cream, vinegar, mustard, curry powder and seasonings to make a dressing.
> Stir the dressing mixture into the pea and cabbage mixture until thoroughly blended.

Oriental Noodle Salad

I served this dish at a East meets West fund-raising luncheon at the Deer Harbor Community Club. It is fun to serve because guests get to create their own salad. I have included a list of favorite ingredients, but you can be creative and add others if you like.

Dressing ingredients:

1/2 cup peanut oil
2 Tablespoons sesame oil
3/4 cup soy sauce
3/4 cup rice wine vinegar
1/3 cup sugar, more to taste

> Combine the above ingredients and set aside.

1 pound Chinese soft noodles
1 Tablespoon sesame oil

Perrenials are the workhorses of the garden, returning year after year with very little effort. Most perrenials will die to the ground for part of the year but a few are evergreen. The first three years of a perrenial's life are usually sleep, creep, and show. Below are some favorite perrenials and their blooming seasons:

Spring - Summer
Bleeding Heart
Cone Flower
Columbine
Forget-Me-Nots
Gladiolus
Peony
Poppy

Summer - Fall
Aster
Day Lily
Hosta
Shasta Daisy

To eat is human
To digest divine.
...Mark Twain

When serving fruit, dip each slice in a water and lemon juice mixture to prevent discoloration.

1/2 cup cooked salad shrimp
1/2 cup cooked ham, cut into julienne
1/2 cup cooked chicken, cut into julienne
1/2 cup cucumbers, thinly sliced
1/2 cup broccoli florets, blanched
1/2 cup cooked green beans, cut into julienne
1 cup shelled green peas, lightly cooked
3/4 cup mushrooms, sliced
1/2 cup radishes, thinly sliced
2 green onions, thinly sliced
2 cups snow peas, blanched with strings removed
1 - 8 ounce can water chestnuts, drained
3 Tablespoons sesame seeds
1/2 cup bean sprouts

> Lightly toast the sesame seeds in a small pan over medium heat. Be sure and keep careful watch, shaking the pan so that they do not burn.

> Cook the Chinese noodles according to package directions. Add the sesame oil to cold water, then drain the noodles and rinse them in it.

> Assemble the toppings in various serving containers. At serving time, heap the noodles in the middle of a platter, surrounded by the toppings. Offer the dressing in a separate pitcher.

Wild Rice Salad

This recipe can be made with any type of rice, adjusting to yields. Orzo also works well.

2 cups water
1 cup wild rice
1 1/2 cups chicken broth
1 clove garlic, peeled but left whole
1 bunch scallions, chopped using some tops
3 Tablespoons butter
1/2 pound chopped mushrooms
3 strips of lean bacon, fried and diced
1/2 cup chopped olives, green or black
3 Tablespoons capers, less with green olives
1/3 cup olive oil
3 Tablespoons tarragon wine vinegar
1/2 teaspoon margoram
1/2 cup sliced celery
1/2 cup chopped walnuts
salt and pepper to taste

>Soak rice in water overnight. Drain. Rinse, then simmer in chicken broth with garlic clove until all liquid is absorbed and the rice is dry but fluffy. Discard garlic.
>In a medium skillet, melt 3 Tablespoons butter and sauté scallions over low heat until soft. Add mushrooms, increase heat and stir until mushrooms begin to soften, but are still firm.
>Remove from heat and add to rice along with remaining ingredients.
>Toss well. Taste for salt and pepper and chill overnight. Mix well before serving.
Serves 6.

Tuna Eggplant Salad

This is an exceptional dish for hot weather. I like to serve it with French bread and Chardonnay.

Wild rice is expensive, but should give a yield of four cups of cooked rice for one cup of uncooked rice. Most other rices will usually yield two cups cooked rice for one cup uncooked rice.
-Susan

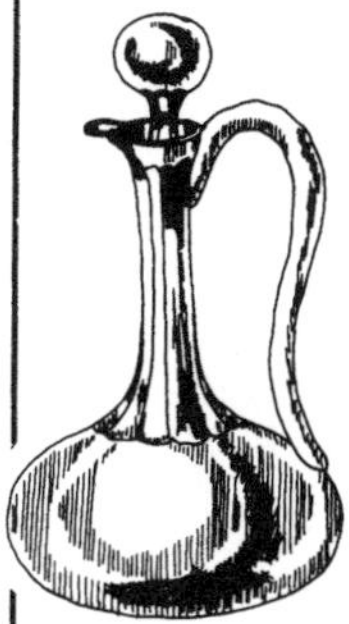

When serving fruit and cheese be aware of the combining of flavors. Apples are tasty with cheddar cubes, pears are lovely with a young Brie or Camembert. Grapes go well with Jack, Jarlsberg or Gruyère.
-Susan

Mulch is a valuable asset to any garden, chiefly because it helps maintain the moisture content of the soil. One way to mulch is to place newspapers or paper grocery bags between the rows in your garden. Then weigh the papers down with hay or grass clippings. The mulch will decompose by the following season and add extra nutrients to the soil as it does.

There are no shortcuts to any place worth going.
- Beverly Sills

1 eggplant, unpeeled but cut into cubes
3 cloves garlic, mashed
6 Tablespoons olive oil
1 - 6 1/2 ounce can water packed white tuna
1 cup sliced olives, green or black (optional)
1/2 cup sunflower seeds
10 cherry tomatoes
1 red pepper, diced
1 medium red onion, chopped
2 ribs celery, diced
3/4 cup yogurt
1/2 cup mayonnaise
1 teaspoon oregano
1 teaspoon basil
salt and pepper

>Sprinkle eggplant with 1 teaspoon salt and let it drain for an hour in a colander.

>Drain and flake tuna.

>Sauté half of the eggplant and half of the minced garlic in 3 Tablespoons olive oil until brown, stirring often. This will take about 7 minutes. Set aside in a bowl and repeat with remaining eggplant, garlic and the remaining Tablespoons of olive oil.

>Remove eggplant with slotted spoon and combine both batches with remaining ingredients,except yogurt, mayonnaise and herbs. Chill at least 3 hours.

>Before serving, mix the yogurt, mayonnaise, oregano and basil to make dressing.

>Fold dressing into tuna-eggplant mixture.

>Season to taste. Serve on a bed of lettuce.

Serves 4.

Pasta Primavera Salad

1 bunch broccoli florets
1 bunch cauliflorets
1 zucchini sliced
1 summer squash, cubed
1 cup green beans, cut
1/2 cup peas
1 pound vermicelli
2 Tablespoons butter
2 cloves garlic, minced
1 bunch scallions, chopped
1 cup mushrooms, thinly sliced
1/4 cup parsely, chopped
2 Tablespoons fresh basil, chopped
2 cups cherry tomatoes, cut into halves
oil and vinegar dressing

>Steam each of the vegetables separately until barely tender, 1 - 2 minutes each.
>After cooking, plunge into cold water to stop the cooking process. The vegetables should be crisp. Refrigerate in plastic bags.
>Cook vermicelli al dente. Rinse under cold water and drain. Set aside.
>Sauté garlic and scallions in butter until limp, but not colored.
>Add mushrooms and stir well to coat. Mushrooms should be slightly limp.
>Mix mushrooms, garlic and scallions with vegetables and pasta.
>Add parsley, basil and tomatoes. Combine and chill.
>Just before serving, add dressing and toss.
Serves 4 to 6.

Planting a garden around a central theme can add to the fun. Here are some ideas for specialty gardens:
Assorted Herbs
Azaleas - Rhododendron
Delphinium
All one color flowers
English Cottage
Wildflowers
Shade loving plants
Summer bulbs
Bird attracting plants
Butterfly attracting plants
Salad Greens
A Calendar Cut-Flower
A Container Garden
A Water Garden

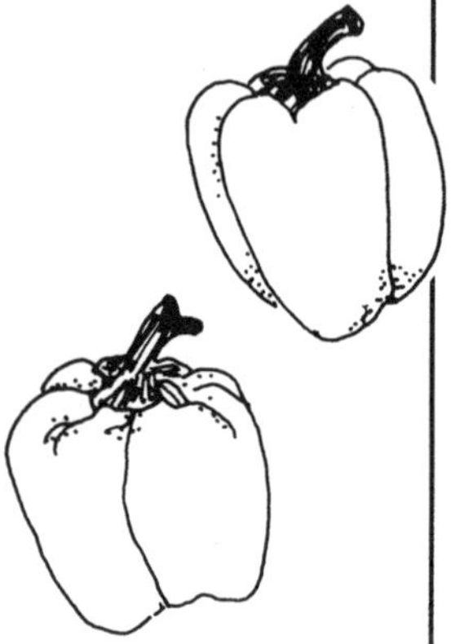

The shortest distance between two points is usually under construction.
- Noelie Alito

Salad Niçoise

This dish is an often prepared favorite. It is equally at home in a buffet at Christmas time or as a full course anytime else.

2 pounds small red potatoes, cooked
2 cups green beans, cooked al dente
2 cups cherry tomatoes
1 cup pitted black olives
1 large green bell pepper, cut into rings, blanched
1 large red bell peppers, cut into rings, blanched
3 carrots, cooked al dente
8 mushrooms, thickly sliced
1 bunch radishes
3 - 7 ounce cans water packed white tuna
salad greens
1 can anchovies (optional)
1 cup cooked artichoke hearts
6 hard boiled eggs, quartered

Dressing:

2 cups olive oil
1/2 cup wine vinegar
1/4 cup lemon juice
2 cloves garlic, crushed
1 Tablespoon dry mustard
1 teaspoon sugar
salt and fresh ground pepper, to taste

> Marinade potatoes, beans, mushrooms, carrots, and artichoke hearts in dressing for a couple of hours.

> Line a large platter with salad greens. Drain vegetables, reserving marinade. Place tuna in the center of the platter and surround with marinaded vegetables.

> Sprinkle with parsley. Serve with dressing on the side.

Favorite Dressing

juice of one lemon
3 Tablespoons white wine vinegar or 2 Tablespoons Balsamic vinegar
pinch of thyme
salt and pepper to taste
up to 3/4 cup of salad or olive oil

>Blend together all ingredients except oil.
>Add oil to personal preference.

Crêpe Filling

I like to make chicken or seafood crêpes for lunch. When served with a salad they make a complete meal. Basic crêpe recipe is on page 33.

1/4 cup butter
1/4 cup flour
1 cup milk
1/2 cup chicken broth
1/2 cup sherry
1/4 cup grated Parmesan cheese
2 Tablespoons shredded raw milk cheddar <u>or</u> swiss
nutmeg, cayenne pepper and salt to taste
1 1/2 pounds, crabmeat, shrimp or cubed chicken

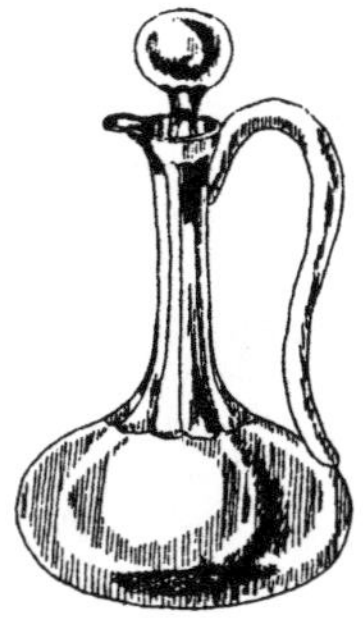

Other additions to salad dressings:

Dijon mustard in small amounts adds a savory spicy depth.

Citrus can replace all or part of the vinegar with excellent results.

Cream or yogurt can add substance to a dressing.

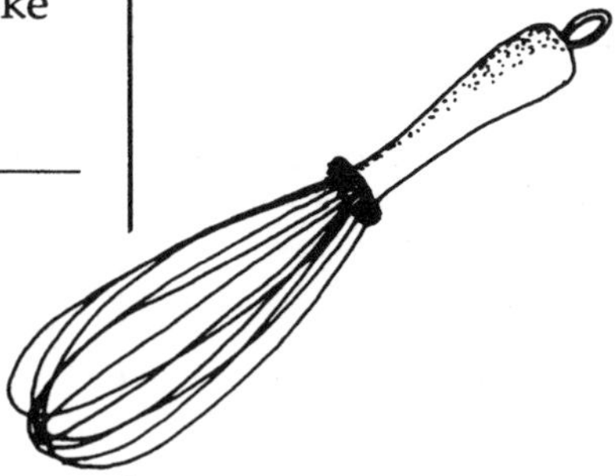

Tips for Flowering Bulbs
In warmer areas, you need to give bulbs an artificial cold period to simulate winter. Place bulbs in the refrigerator for about 8 weeks to trick them into dormancy. But you must keep fruit out of the refrigerator during this time. Ripening fruit produces ethylene, a gas that will stop bulbs from flowering.

>In a saucepan melt the butter and stir in the flour.

>Whisk in the milk and chicken broth and cook until thickened.

>Add sherry, cheeses, nutmeg, pepper and salt. Heat until cheeses melt and remove from heat. At this point, the sauce can be refrigerated.

>When you are ready to fill your crêpes, make enough crêpes so that each person will have two.

>Cook the crabmeat, shrimp or chicken for the filling. Mix half of the sauce with your choice of filling.

>Preheat oven to 350°.

>Spoon a portion of the filling down the center of each crêpe and fold the sides into the center. Place filled crêpes in an oven proof dish, folded side down. Cover with the remaining sauce and sprinkle with Parmesan cheese, if desired. Put into oven at 350° until heated thoroughly.

Serves 8.

Spiced Cider with Apple Brandy

2 broken cinnamon sticks
1 Tablespoon allspice berries
3 cloves
1 quart apple cider or apple juice
3/4 cup apple brandy (Calvados) or apple-jack
6 cinnamon sticks (for serving)

> Tie the spices in a cheesecloth bag. Place in

a 2-quart pot and add the cider. Heat slowly until hot but not boiling.
> Put 1 cinnamon stick and 1 ounce brandy in each of 6 mugs.
> Pour cider in each mug and stir with the cinnamon stick to blend.
> Serve immediately.

Serves 6.

Holiday Punch

one fifth Southern Comfort
2 bottles champagne
1 bottle club soda
1 cup cranberry juice
3/4 cup lemon juice

> The day before, freeze the cranberry juice overnight in ice rings.
> Mix together in a punch bowl; Southern Comfort, soda, lemon juice. Add champagne last.
> Add cranberry juice rings as decoration. Serve immediately.

Favorite Toasts

May you be granted health, wealth and happiness and the wisdom to enjoy them all.

* * * *

May your memories of the past bring you as much pleasure as your anticipation of the future.

* * * *

May you always have many friends; old ones to help you grow old and new ones to help you stay young.

* * * *

May the celebration of life forever sing in your ears.

Flower Cuisine

Whenever possible, use garden grown flowers, they offer the greatest fragrance and taste. As a general rule, flowers should be gathered in early morning, washed and refrigerated until used. Flowers which are to be dried, however, should be picked at midday when they are free from moisture. Always wash flowers gently, but thoroughly before use.

Borage - Clusters of small, blue, star-shaped flowers with a rough gray foliage. Flourishes in ordinary soil, very easily grown and a great attracter of bees. Honeyed cucumber taste, a beautiful garnish.

Carnation - Large, originally a pale pink in color, now deep red. Commonly used in wines and the liqueur Chartreuse. Clovelike in flavor and fragrance.

Chrysanthemum - Large, bold, yellow with heavy petals. Originated in China 500 B.C. Aromatic piquant flavor, best in soups and salads.

Dandelion - Small yellow flowers, dark green leaves. Originated in Greece, Native Americans used it as a medicinal. Young leaves can be cooked and served like spinach, made into a salad, or boiled into tea.

Gardenia - Soft, delicate white flowers. Grown in warm climates. Vivid, sweet fragrance. Good for candied flowers.

Gladiolus - Many colored varieties, sword-like leaves. Similar to lettuce in flavor, good in salads, beautiful as a garnish.

Lavender - Small, violet flowers, of the mint family, very sweet aroma. Commonly used by herbalists; good in soups, salads, teas.

Marigold - Large, golden flower with many petals. Very hardy, easy to grow. Mild pleasant, peppery flavor. Commonly used as a flavoring to baked goods and for coloring.

Nasturtium - Variety of colors. Originated in Peru. Easy to grow, but needs sun. Light peppery flavor similar to cress. Good for salads and garnishes.

Pansy - Deep hues, velvety, face-like flower. Has no distinctive flavor. Best as a garnish.

Rose - Use the petals only. High in vitamin C. Good for a large variety of uses including teas, jelly, candy, salads, garnish.

Violet - Small, fragrant, white, blue, purple or yellow petals. Readily gives up color and flavor when boiled. High in vitamin C. Good in salads, teas and as a garnish.

Cheeses

Since Washington is first among all 50 states in milk production, a thriving cheese industry exists there. And the cuisine-conscious producers do not stop with cheese made from cow's milk, but use goat's and sheep's milk as well.

Commercial cheesemaking in the Pacific Northwest began in Tillamook, Oregon in 1899 and focused on the traditional cheeses such as cheddar, colby and Swiss. Today there is a wide selection of cheeses including Quark, a soft yogurt/cream cheese mixture, and a variety of cheddar cheeses with flavorings of linguisa or chorizo added.

Some of the limited-production Washington cheeses are sold in supermarkets, sometimes under regional rather than brand names. If your supermarket does carry a particular type, look in specialty cheese shops, fancy food stores and health-food stores throughout the area.

Below are some cheeses and their uses.

Blue - French origin; tangy sharp; appetizer, salad and dessert.

Cheddar - English origin; mild to very sharp; snack, cooking and dessert.

Edam, Gouda - Dutch origin; mild; appetizer, snack and dessert.

Provolone - Italian origin; can be smoked; mild to sharp; cooking and snack.

Brie - French origin; mild to pungent; appetizer, dessert.

Cream - U.S. origin; very mild, chill slightly; salads, snacks and dessert.

Ricotta - Italian origin; mild, curd or dry; cooking and dessert.

Mozzarella - Italian origin; mild; cooking, snacks.

Roquefort - French origin; sharp, salty; appetizer, salad and dessert.

Swiss - mild, nutty, sweet flavor; appetizer, sandwich, cooking and dessert.

Monterey - California origin; mild; appetizer, cooking, sandwich.

Pacific Northwest Shellfish

Clams - There are two kinds of clams; littleneck and longneck. Of the littleneck clams, the most common are the native littleneck and the Manila clam, a littleneck that was imported to the Pacific Northwest from Japan. A rapid and hardy breeder, Manilas settled into a ecological niche and are now the bulk of the Pacific Northwest clam industry. Steaming is the most popular method of cooking either clam and the debate over which is sweeter or better goes on. But the Manila is the more attractive of the two with beautiful black stripes which contrast with the dull shell of the native littleneck.

The most famous of Northwest clams is probably the Geoduck, pronounced "Gooey-duck." A distinctive longneck, the Geoduck often weighs several pounds and makes a delicious clam chowder. Sushi bars serve part of this clam as "Giant Clam," but to Northwesterners, it will always be Geoduck.

Oysters - An oyster is not an oyster is not an oyster. People everywhere have their favorites and swear by them. Some oysters which grow in one part of the world will not grow in others. Although they are common in Northwest markets and restaurants, the oyster most often grown on the Eastern Seaboard will not grow at all in the Pacific Northwest. Here are the best known Northwest varieties.

Olympia - Pacific Northwest natives, the tiny Olympia oysters are grown in South Puget Sound. Although mild of flavor, this oyster has a metallic aftertaste.

Belon - Also known as European flat oysters, these are the most like those grown in Maine.

If the environment is the meat and potatoes of a place, then the people who live there are the seasonings. Sometimes, tourists do not notice the residents of a community. They admire the quaint gift shop, how clean the beach is, or the chummy atmosphere in the café at lunch, but do not give much thought to the people who create and flavor these spots.

Without realizing it, tourists often are drawn to a place by the spirit of the locals, people they rarely bother to know. Travelers, on the other hand, are aware that local residents have as much to offer a visitor as the land itself. Travelers wonder how someone can visit a place and not notice the people who live there. We liken it to dating a girl because she is pretty, but not talking to her because what she thinks does not interest you.

When you travel to a new area, you have a date with everyone who lives there. Orcas is certainly an attractive companion but, if you look beneath the surface, you will find it is filled with character as well. If the island is a great place to visit, the residents make it that way. They are the ones who work to insure that the island retains its distinctive personality. They are not the clean up crew or entertainment operators, but the people whose home you are visiting. Their personalities create the charm visitors so admire.

Most of the islanders that visitors get to know are introduced through something that they do. A noteable example is John Trumbull. John is a baker extraordinaire who opened a combination bakery and cafe a few years back. In the heart of town, Rose's Cafe soon became a favorite with both locals and visitors. John sold the cafe to two sisters, who changed the name to the Comet Cafe, but kept the quality fare for which John had become locally famous. John maintains the bakery end of the business and has added a wide range of thoughtfully selected domestic and imported wines, specialty cheeses and meats, and a wonderful array of take home food. You will note John's contribution to this book right after the dinner section.

Lila and Irv Berman are a couple you might notice in the bakery. Lila, a retired therapist, and Irv, a former civil engineer, have traveled over most of the globe, but still think that John's sour dough baguettes are some of the best they have ever eaten. The Bermans like to spend time at the library and they are great fans of Boggle. Lila is one of the locals who enjoys acting in productions put on by the community theater, but she still finds time to be on the board of Hospice.

Cy Fraser shares the Berman's appreciation of Orcas Island Community Theater. But, he also donates large amounts of his time to the Eastsound Planning Commission. You might find him around town, talking to residents about where they think the next street should go, or you might find him cooking at his restaurant, Bilbo's. A Mexican restaurant that has been praised in many publications, Bilbo's dining reflects the island's spirit. Everything is fresh, locally grown when possible, and the atmosphere is relaxed and festive. Even though Cy's business is partially supported by tourists, he does not believe in promotional tourism. "Beauty," he says, "is best discovered, not advertised."

Across the street from Bilbo's is Teezer's, a great place for lunch or homemade cookies. Teezer's is owned by Carolyn and Mark Bledsoe, but the name comes from the fact that Carolyn and her sisters; Lisa, Sandie and Louise, all began life as Ortizes. Of Mexican heritage, all the sisters have worked at Bilbo's at one time or another. Carolyn has been an active volunteer in the school. In past years, she has been among the driving forces for the school's annual Holiday Fair, a major fun and fund raiser. The fair is organized by the Orcas Island Education Foundation, a non-profit organization.

The impetus behind the Orcas Island Education Foundation

was Kathy Youngren. Kathy no longer serves on the district schoolboard, but her family, husband Jim and sons Brent, Eric and Andrew, operate a non-profit salmon enhancement project on their property. Jim also began and supports Chick and Egg Production, a major funder of the Children's Trust Foundation. The Trust Foundation is a child abuse prevention organization based in Seattle. Chick and Egg Productions produces hand-crafted wooden furniture for children and adults. The young fir poles used in this furniture are cut on Orcas Island and sent to Seattle. The organization's name comes from the idea that child abuse is a cycle, that abused children often grow up to be abusive parents.

The Bawden's family business is oysters and mussels, raised in their beds at Judd Cove Shellfish. Bill Bawden has an intense love of fish of any kind and has been involved with some sort of fish market for as far back as he cares to remember. A native of the south, Bill has a strong drawl and a wiry sense of humor. Char, the other half of the Bawden family business, shares some of her favorite oyster recipes later in the book.

Scattered among the other island residents, quietly serving you in a restuarant, or guiding you on a kayak tour, or teaching yoga at a Westsound studio, are artists and craftspeople. They fill the Artworks with pottery, or knitted sweaters, or paintings. They were drawn to Orcas because its peacefulness and natural beauty inspire their art, whatever form it may take. Unless you ask, you may never know how talented they are.

There are many people with hidden talents in all communities. They quietly pick up litter on the roadway, go out of their way to be helpful to visitors, or donate their time and money to charities. What these people and Orcas Island residents have in common is that they love where they live. They love it enough that they have shaped their lives around supporting local standards. But they have done it in style, maintaining their individuality. That is what feeds all communities. Individuals, as well as natural scenic beauty, are an area's treasures. That is what feeds a community and makes it unique.

Chewing on a bit of fresh parsley or mint will help eliminate the smell of just eaten garlic.

Fresh herbs lose their distinctive flavor when cooked a long time. Add some extra just before serving to enhance the flavor.

Salad Greens Chart

The best salads are mixed with more than one type of green. When mixed with the many types of vinaigrettes, the combinations are endless. Below are a few types of salad greens:

Arugula - intense and pungent
Belgian Endive - crisp and opalescent
Bibb Lettuce - crunchy and sweet
Dandelion Greens - tart, must be young and tender
Escarole - yellow/white, pleasantly tart
Fennel Greens - use just the tips, Anise flavored
Leaf lettuce - red or green, best when young
Nasturtium leaves - peppery, use sparingly
Radiccio - small and ruby red, slightly bitter
Romaine - robust and nutty
Sorrel - tart and slightly acidic
Spinach - blends well with many greens
Watercress - spicy and deep green

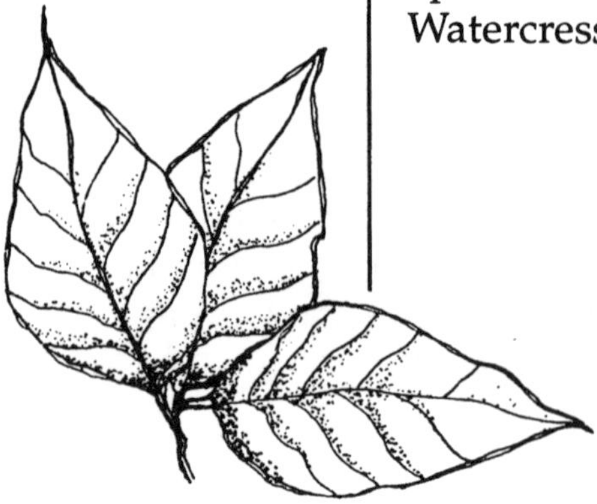

My personal preference in cookbooks is for those which provide me with menus. Most cookbook authors, having made the dish several times, have experimented with the flavors and textures that surround a dish. I appreciate the suggestions about what they feel is the best possible combination. Also I enjoy the opportunity to peak inside their heads and have a chance to see their preferences. Knowing their tastes better, I understand more what they intended the dish to be.

With that in mind, I have provided menus in this section. These menus are prepared for four people unless otherwise noted. If the recipe doesn't follow, page numbers are given for convenience.

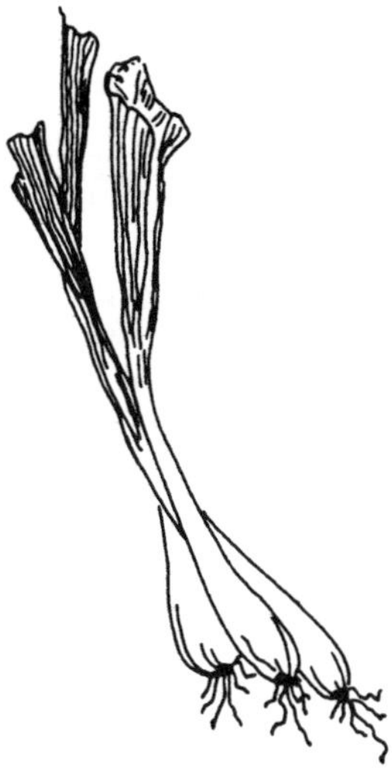

Crown Roast of Pork Dinner
Mushroom Soup - page 80.
Crown Roast of Pork with Mustard Sauce
Wild Rice and Cranberry Stuffing
Spinach or Chard with Tomato and Garlic
Green Salad
Ice Cream Torte - page 173.

Crown Roast of Pork with Stuffing

1 crown roast of pork

>Preheat oven to 350°.
>Trim roast well. Cover the bone ends with foil. Fit another piece of foil under the roast so that the stuffing does not fall out.
>Place in roasting pan and roast in the oven for 20 minutes, per pound.
>One hour before the roast is done, pile stuffing in the center of the roast. Put it back in the oven to continue roasting. After 30 minutes, cover the stuffing with foil so it does not get too brown.

This dish is a favorite at my house and especially nice for holidays and formal dining occasions. It creates a knockout impression and appeals to a wide variety of palates.
-Susan

Stuffing can be made the day before and refrigerated until needed.

-Susan

Although the French are known for their butter laden and cheese filled dishes, they have a lower heart disease rate than Americans, who eat less butter and cheese annually. Baffled experts have purposed several possible explanations for this. Some attribute the healthy French heart to the low stress life style they enjoy. Others think it may be the result of consuming wine with their meals.

"Viva la France!" the response of Orcas Island resident Carol Wright after being informed of the above.

>To serve, place roast on serving platter, leaving foil underneath the roast, but removing foil covers on the bone ends. Serve with mustard sauce.

Wild Rice and Cranberry Stuffing

4 cups wild rice, cooked according to package directions
2 cups raw cranberries, coarsely chopped
1/2 cup butter, melted
2 Tablespoons onion, finely chopped
1 teaspoon salt
3 Tablespoons sugar
1/2 teaspoon marjoram
1 clove garlic, minced
1/2 teaspoon mace
1/2 teaspoon thyme
1/2 teaspoon dill
1/2 teaspoon pepper

>Sauté onion in butter for two minutes or until tender.
>Add seasoning and stir until well blended. Cook for two more minutes.
>Stir in remaining ingredients and cook until thoroughly heated, about 10 minutes.
>Let cool.

Mustard Sauce

This sauce is also good with beef or lamb.

4 Tablespoons pan drippings or butter
3 Tablespoons flour
1 cup dry white wine
1/2 cup chicken or beef broth
1/4 cup whipping cream
3 Tablespoons dijon mustard
1 teaspoon dry mustard
salt & pepper

>In a large saucepan, cook flour in the drippings or butter over low heat until lightly colored, about 3 minutes.
>Add wine and broth and cook for 5 minutes or until thickened.
>Add cream and mustard. Cook very slowly for 2 more minutes. Season to taste.
>Serve warm with roast.

When roasting meat, allow the meat to remain uncovered to retain its juices. If a rich gravy is desired, place meat in a covered pan or dish.

If you haven't the strength to impose your own terms upon life, you must accept the terms that it offers you.
. . . T. S. Eliot

Spinach with Garlic and Tomato

1 large bunch fresh spinach or chard
2 cloves minced garlic
1 can solid packed or stewed tomatoes

>Wash and remove stems, chop the spinach or chard. Put in a large pot.
>Add garlic and tomatoes. Heat slowly and thoroughly.
>Serve with a slotted spoon so the vegetable is not soupy.

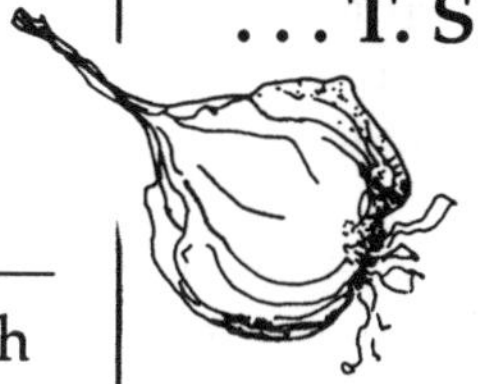

Chard may be substituted in any recipe calling for spinach.
-Susan

Lamb Dinner Menu

Tomato Toasts
Cauliflower Soup - page 81.
Butterflied Leg of Lamb with
Cumberland Sauce
Apple Chutney
Kate's Rice
Spinach Timbale
Green Salad
Chocolate Mousse - page 168.

You can tell when steaks and chops are cooked by the appearance of small drops of blood on the uncooked side of the meat. At that point turn the meat and wait again for the juice to appear in small droplets which is a signal that the meat is cooked. Do not use a fork to turn the meat. Use tongs, or a firm wide spatula. If the meat is pricked with the tines of a fork, juices will be lost.

Tomato Toasts

12 tomato slices
12 thinly sliced pieces of French bread
1 cup mayonnaise
2 garlic cloves, minced

>Mix mayonnaise with minced garlic.
>Put one tomato slice on each slice of bread top with a dollop of garlic mayonnaise.
>Broil until mayonnaise is lightly browned.
>Serve hot.

Butterflied Leg of Lamb

1 leg of lamb, boned
1 cup olive oil
1/4 cup dry Vermouth
1 Tablespoon oregano
2 cloves garlic, peeled and sliced
1 onion, peeled and cut into eighths

1 dozen peppercorns

>Mix all the ingredients in a large bowl except for the lamb.
>Trim most of the fat from the lamb and marinate in the mixture for at least 4 hours. Turn the meat often.
>Barbecue over hot coals for 45 minutes or until pink.
>Slice and serve with Cumberland Sauce.

Cumberland Sauce

1/2 cup water
1/2 cup port wine
2 Tablespoons red currant jelly
1/2 teaspoon dijon mustard
pinch cayenne
juice of 1 lemon, save the rind
juice of 1 orange, save the rind

>Slice and chop rinds of the orange and the lemon. Boil with 1/2 cup water for 5 minutes. Strain and discard rind.
>Add remaining ingredients and boil for 4 minutes. Cool.
>Serve in a sauce dish.

When hamburger stands began cropping up in Rome a few years ago, wine and food writer, Carlo Petrini became concerned about Italy's gastronomic culture. In defense he founded the *Slow Food Foundation,* dedicated to eating slowly and savoring the moment. Based on the principles that fast food is an impoverishment of a culture and that meals are the only time people in most cultures have to meet and talk, *Slow Food* has now mushroomed in membership in 27 countries and has expanded its agenda to encouraging the banning of pesticides and condemning the deforestation of the Amazon for the purpose of raising cattle.

Chutneys are relishes made with fruits and preserved with sugar, vinegar and spices. They originated in medieval times, giving spark to breads and cheeses. Chutneys are also wonderful compliments to meat dishes, adding color and zest to a meal.

Always stir rice with a fork. Using a spoon bruises the grains and makes them sticky.

Apple Chutney

20 tart apples
3/4 pound raisins
3/4 pound currants
6 ounces chopped citrus peel
1/4 cup crushed hot peppers
1/4 cup chopped fresh ginger root
1/8 cup minced garlic
2 large onions, chopped fine
1/4 cup preserved ginger, chopped fine
3 pounds sugar
1 1/2 quarts vinegar
1/2 Tablespoon ground ginger
1/2 Tablespoon cumin
1/2 Tablespoon nutmeg
10 pint canning jars

>Bring sugar and vinegar to a boil. Add spices and the remainder of the ingredients. Bring to a boil again and cook over a very low heat for 4 to 5 hours, or until quite thick. Stir occasionally.

>Pack in canning jars according to manufacturer's directions.

Yield: 10 pints

Kate's Rice

1 cup uncooked rice
1/2 cup butter
4 scallions, sliced thinly, tops too
6 mushrooms, sliced
1 Tablespoon oregano

1 can bouillon
2 cups water

>Preheat oven to 350°.
>Sauté rice in butter until lightly colored.
>Add scallions, mushrooms and oregano. Sauté together for 5 minutes.
>Add bouillon and water. Pour into covered baking dish and bake for 1 hour or until all liquid is absorbed.

Never eat more than you can lift.
. . . Miss Piggy

Spinach Timbale

2-3 bunches fresh spinach, cleaned, stemmed, chopped and blanched
4 Tablespoons minced shallots
3 Tablespoons butter
1/3 cup heavy cream
freshly ground nutmeg
salt
pepper
3 eggs

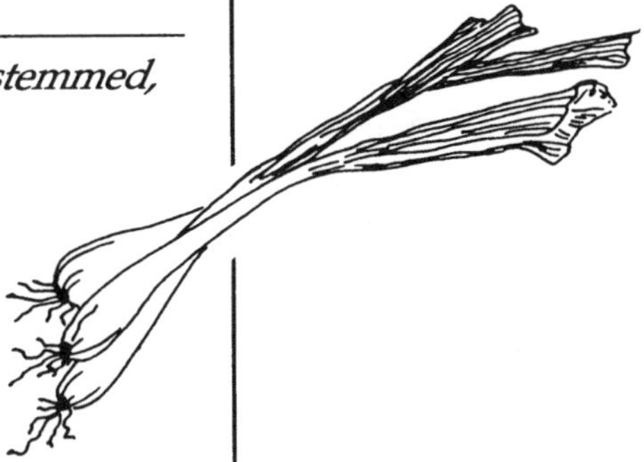

>Preheat oven to 325°.
>Sauté shallots in butter until limp.
>In a food processor with a metal blade, purée the well dried, blanched spinach with the cream. Add nutmeg, salt and pepper to taste. With the motor running, add one egg at a time and blend for about 3 seconds.
>Divide the mixture between six well-buttered 3/4 cup oven-proof molds. Timbale molds work the best, but if you do not have any, use oven-proof custard cups or individual soufflé bowls.
>Cover each mold with a well buttered

Soufflé is a French word meaning "a puff of wind." The term is used in both cooking and ceramics. Without the accent over the "e", it is a medical term. In cooking it refers to any of several baked foods made light and puffy by the addition of beaten egg whites before baking.

square of foil.
>Place the molds in a deep pan filled with water halfway up the sides of the molds.
>Bake for 25-30 minutes, or until a small knife inserted in the center of one of the molds comes out clean.
>Remove from oven and pan of water and let set for 5 minutes.
>Turn upside down on plates and unmold.

English Pub Dinner Menu
Scotch Eggs
Pickled Onions
Potted Shrimp
Steak and Kidney Pie
Composted Salad
Pavlova - page 163.
Beer

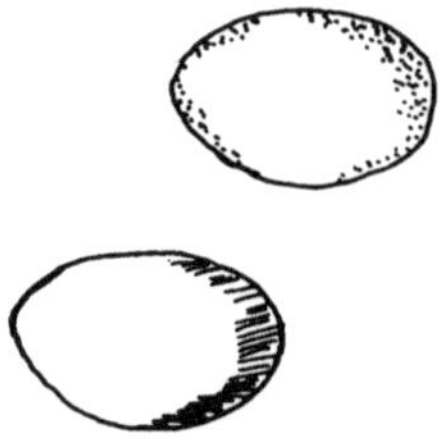

To keep eggs from cracking while boiling, make a small pin prick in the large end (this is where the air sac is) before adding it to the water.

Scotch Eggs

6 hard boiled eggs, chilled and peeled
1 pound bulk sausage
Fine bread crumbs, roughly an amount equal to the sausage
1 raw egg
1/4 teaspoon anchovy paste
olive oil

>Take out 1/4 cup bread crumbs. Mix the remainder with the sausage.
>Add the raw egg and the anchovy paste to the sausage / bread crumb mixture.
>Roll the peeled eggs in plain bread crumbs.

>Carefully encase each egg in the sausage mixture, about 1/4-1/2 inch thick.
>Deep fry in medium hot oil for 5-6 minutes. Drain well on paper towels.
>Serve with mustard and pickles.

Homemade Mustard (Famous and Secret)

A guest gave Bill this recipe years ago to thank him for making her stay so special. Since that time, I have made this mustard for the school Holiday Fair and it has sold out almost before the fair opened.

8 ounces Coleman's dry mustard
1 cup rice wine vinegar
6 eggs, beaten
1 cup sugar
1/2 stick butter
canning jars

>Soak the mustard in the vinegar for 2 hours.
>Add the eggs and sugar.
>Cook until mixture reaches a boil, stirring occasionally. This scorches very easily, so be diligent.
>Remove from heat and add butter. Stir until butter melts, then seal in canning jars according to manufacturer's directions. This keeps in the refrigerator quite well and must be refrigerated once opened.

A very entertaining cooking teacher in California mixes one bottle of good English stout with 4 bottles of generic beer in a serving pitcher. It takes the taste of the expensive import for a fraction of the price.
-Susan

Seeing is deceiving. It's eating that's believing.
. . . James Thurber

There ain't no surer way to find out if you like people or hate them than to travel with them.
. . . Mark Twain

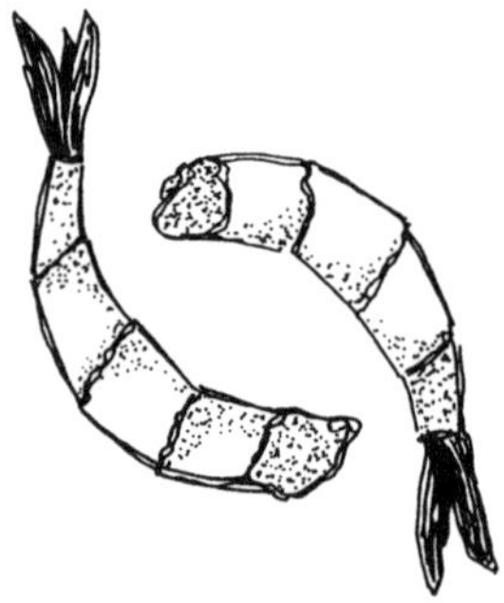

The British believe that a good ale should be served at cellar temperature, around 55°. This is a bit warmer than Americans are used to, but to serve it any chillier, the Brits say, would mask the flavors.

Pickled Onions

2 pounds white onions, not pearl onions, but 1 inch boiling onions
1/2 cup salt
1/2 cup sugar
1/4 cup salt
2 Tablespoons mixed pickling spice
6 - 8 whole cloves of garlic
10 - 12 whole peppercorns
1 quart malt vinegar
wide mouth canning jars or a small crock

>Put onions in a steamer and steam until they can just barely be pierced. Peel, rinse, put in a bowl with 1/2 cup salt and enough cold water to cover. Let sit overnight.
>The next day, simmer 1/4 cup salt with the remaining ingredients. While the mixture is simmering, pack the onions into jars or a small crock. Pour the spicy vinegar mixture over the onions.
>Refrigerate. These onions will keep 4 to 6 weeks.

Potted Shrimp

1/4 pound butter
1/4 teaspoon each mace and nutmeg or 1/2 teaspoon curry powder
pinch cayenne pepper
2 cups very small cooked shrimp
2 teaspoons lemon juice
1 teaspoon onion juice (optional)
clarified butter
packing jars or 2 - 10 ounce crocks

>Melt the butter over medium heat. Add mace and nutmeg or curry powder, and cayenne pepper.
>Add shrimp, lemon juice and onion juice. Stir to coat shrimp.
>Carefully pack, so as not to mash shrimp, into crocks or jars. Allow to cool.
>When cool, pour enough clarified butter over the top of the shrimp mixture to completely cover it. Keep refrigerated.
>Serve as spread for crackers or thin pieces of brown bread.
Makes approximately 2 cups.

Henry VIII found the upper or choice part of the loin of beef so good that he knighted it, thus the word sirloin. This is why it is also called a "Baron of Beef."

Beefsteak and Kidney Pie

3/4 pound top sirloin of beef cut into 1 inch cubes
1/2 pound lamb or beef kidneys
1/4 teaspoon salt
1/4 teaspoon pepper
1/4 teaspoon paprika
1/4 cup all purpose flour
1 medium onion, thinly sliced
2 Tablespoons shortening
2 cups beef stock or 2 cups beef bouillon
1 bay leaf
4 mushrooms, sliced
1 Tablespoon butter
1 pie crust

>10 minutes before the pie is to go into the oven, preheat to 450°.
>Trim any fat or membrane from the beef and kidneys. Cut the kidneys into 1/8 inch thick slices.
>Place the salt, pepper, paprika and flour in a paper bag and shake to mix. Add the

While browning small pieces of meat, do not allow them to touch. This will retain the meat juices in each piece.

Some of the greatest culinary combinations are the simple ones. Be creative, but do not be so busy trying to be different that you hide the flavor of what you are cooking.

-Susan

I do not recommend many vegetable recipes. That is because I believe whole heartedly in fresh vegetables. If you begin with fresh ingredients, steam them lightly and serve them with a minimum of seasonings and butter, that is the best way to prepare them for flavor and nutrition.

-Susan

beef, kidney and onions and shake until well coated.

>Melt the shortening in a large skillet or dutch oven. Let it get very hot, then add the beef, kidney and onions.

>Sauté, over high heat, stirring constantly, until the meat is brown. Add the stock and bay leaf.

>Reduce the heat to low, cover the skillet and simmer 1 hour or until tender.

>Remove from the heat and discard the bay leaf. Cool. Place the mixture in a 1 1/2 quart baking dish.

>Sauté the sliced mushrooms in butter and put on top of the meat mixture.

>Roll out the pie crust and cover the pie, sealing the edges of the casserole. Cut vents for the steam to escape.

>Bake for 10-15 minutes at 450°, then reduce to 350° and bake an additional 15-20 minutes or until the crust is golden brown.

Composted Salad

1/2 pound broccoli
1 package frozen green peas
1 cup diagonally sliced celery
1/2 cup sliced radishes
1 cup cherry tomatoes
1 cucumber, sliced
1 head lettuce
salad dressing

>Cook broccoli in boiling water until just tender. Put under cold running water to stop the cooking action.

>Cook peas until just tender and cool under cold water also.

>Put broccoli, peas and the remaining ingredients, except the lettuce and dressing, in a large bowl. Cover with your favorite dressing and chill for 1 hour.
>When ready to serve, tear the lettuce, mix with the vegetables, toss and serve.

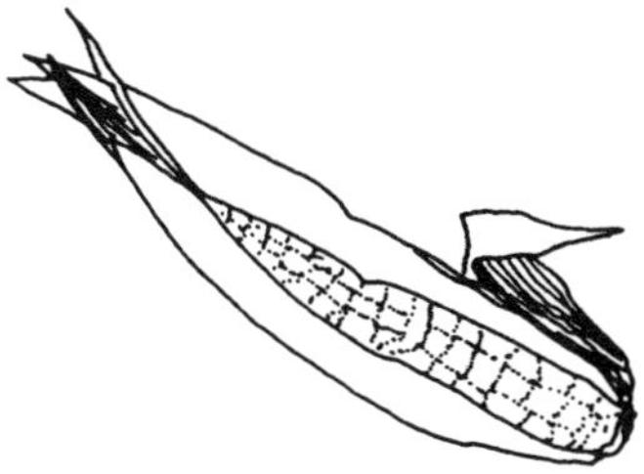

Fiesta Dinner Menu
Gazpacho - page 79.
Tamale Corn Pie
Corn Tortillas
Your Own Avacado Salad
Orange cake - page 158.

Tamale Corn Pie

This recipe can be made and stored uncooked and covered in the refrigerator or freezer for several days.

1 chicken, cooked
4 large tamales, chicken or chicken and turkey
1 can creamed corn
1 - 4 ounce can chopped green chilies
15 medium or large black olives, cut into thirds
1 pound Martin's New York cheese or raw milk cheddar

>Preheat oven to 350°.
>Skin chicken and remove meat from bones. Cut meat into chunks.
>Defrost and crush tamales. Put into a large mixing bowl. Add remaining ingredients except cheese. Mix to blend.
>Put 1/3 of the cheese in the bottom of an

This is a fun dinner, but must be made in advance. You will want to make the Tamale Corn and the Gazpacho the day before you plan on serving them. If you are serving guests, this gives you more time with them and less time in the kitchen.

In the Northwest, there is not a large variety of tamales available. I use Garibaldi 11 ounce turkey and chicken tamales, which I found in the frozen food section at Safeway.
-Susan

oven-proof casserole. Add 1/2 tamale mixture. Put another 1/3 cheese over the tamale mixture, then add remaining tamale mixture. Top with remaining cheese.
>Cook at 350° until smooth and bubbly.
>Serve with salsa, sour cream and garnish with cilantro.

Fish Dinner Menu
Oysters with Leek Purée
Mushroom Soup - page 80.
Fresh Fish Parmesan
Scalloped Potatoes
Squash Purée
Strawberry Supreme - page 171.

Have you ever wondered why most cookbooks contain recipes for rice, noodles and potatoes? This is because many chefs consider these starchs the ideal accompaniment for main courses.

Oysters with Leek Purée

1 bunch leeks
1/2 cup water
1 cup dry white wine
1/2 teaspoon salt
8 Tablespoons unsalted butter
1/4 teaspoon white pepper
2 dozen fresh oysters in the shell
rock salt as needed

>Clean the leeks. Reserve a few pieces of the dark green portion for garnish. Slice the remainder, using the white and creamy green portion only.
>Simmer leeks, water, wine, salt and 4 Table-spoons of butter in a covered sauce pan for 45 minutes. Leeks should be very soft with

a syrupy glaze. Simmer uncovered for a few minutes to reduce the remaining liquid.
>Purée in a food processor and beat in the remaining 4 Tablespoons of butter, cut into small bits.
>Blanch a few strips of the dark green leek tops in boiling water for 30 seconds, then rinse in cold water to stop the cooking process. Drain, dry and reserve.
>All the above steps may be done a day or two in advance. If you are preparing in advance, refrigerate at this stage.
>Prior to serving, preheat oven to 500°.Open oysters and arrange each on its half shell in rock salt spread on an ovenproof platter or plate. Be careful not to spill any of the oyster liquor.
>Put the leek purée on top of each oyster. Bake for 5 minutes, then put under a broiler for a minute to glaze the purée.
>Garnish each oyster with a piece of the green leek top and serve immediately.

Sometimes the most urgent and vital thing you can possibly do is take a complete rest.
. . . Ashleigh Brilliant

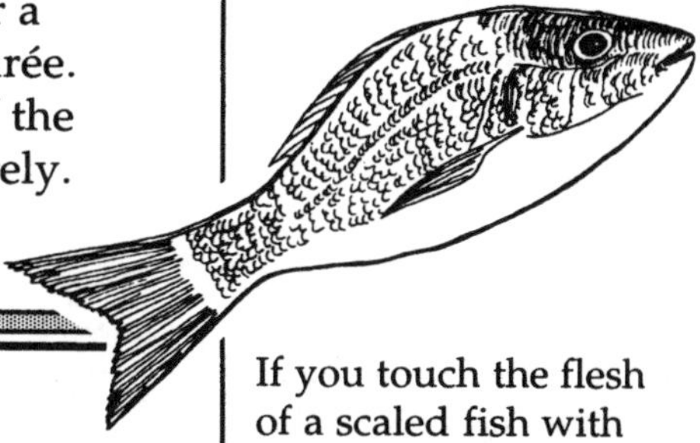

If you touch the flesh of a scaled fish with your fingers and no impression remains, this is a sign of freshness. A fresh fish has no unpleasant odor and is never slimy. A piece of fresh fish will smell of the sea.

Fresh Fish Parmesan

2 pounds red snapper, cod, or other firm white fish
1 Tablespoon lemon juice
1 Tablespoon Worcestershire sauce
1/2 cup flour
3 eggs, lightly beaten
1 cup freshly grated Parmesan or Romano cheese
3 Tablespoons butter
2 Tablespoons vegetable oil

Sometimes you have to travel far from home to appreciate how to prepare the local bounty.
. . .Tom Stockley

When making mashed potatoes use hot milk, or the liquid they were cooked in, cold liquid will make them heavy or soggy. For fluffier mashed potatoes add a pinch of baking soda along with the milk and butter.

>Cut fish into serving pieces and put into a bowl.
>Sprinkle the Worcestershire sauce and lemon juice over the fillets and turn to coat. Salt and pepper each piece and dredge them in flour.
>Dip fillets into the beaten egg to coat, then cover with a coating of the grated cheese.
>Heat butter and oil in a frying skillet and sauté on each side until brown.
>If the fillets are thick, place the skillet in a 400° oven for 5 minutes to finish cooking.
>Serve immediately.

Creamy Scalloped Potatoes

6 large potatoes
1 medium onion, finely chopped
3 Tablespoons flour
1/4 cup butter
3 cups half & half
1 teaspoon dried thyme
1 Tablespoon parsley, chopped
salt
pepper

>Preheat oven to 350°.
>Wash potatoes, leaving skins on. Cut cross ways into thin slices.
>Butter a 2 quart baking dish. Arrange 1/3 of the potatoes in the bottom of the dish. Top with a dot of butter, a sprinkle of seasonings, a sprinkle of onions and 1 Tablespoon of flour. Alternate a layer of potatoes and a layer of butter, seasonings, flour and onion

until all are used.
>Pour the half & half over the potatoes.
>Cover the dish and bake for 30 minutes. Then uncover and bake for 50 minutes longer or until potatoes are tender.
>Let stand 5 to 10 minutes before serving.

Purée of Zucchini and Yellow Squash

3/4 pound zucchini
3/4 pound yellow squash
1/2 cup chopped onion
1 clove garlic, minced
3 Tablespoons butter
1/2 cup dry white wine
1/2 cup water
1 teaspoon thyme
1 teaspoon oregano

>Sauté onion and garlic in butter until limp. Add chopped zucchini, chopped yellow squash, wine and water. Steam until vegetables are tender, adding a little water if necessary. Watch carefully as they will cook quickly and you do not want to scorch the vegetables.
>When soft, put into a food processor with a metal blade, juice and all, and process with salt, pepper, thyme and oregano. Process until almost smooth.
>Serve in individual au gratin dishes.

Steam or stir fry vegetables whenever possible to avoid losing flavor and vitamins. If you do boil vegetables, bring the water to a boil before you drop them in. Never let vegetables stand in cold water before cooking. The less exposure to air and water that the vegetable gets, the better. Prepare the vegetables as close to cooking time as possible or cook them whole and slice after they are cooked.

Mussel Dinner Menu
Mussels in Cream
Green Salad
Sourdough French Bread - page 56.
Fresh Fruit Sorbet - page 172.

Mussels are very rich, especially when prepared with a wine/cream sauce. This may be offered as the first course of a very fancy dinner or makes a delicious but simple dinner when served with the menu above.
-Susan

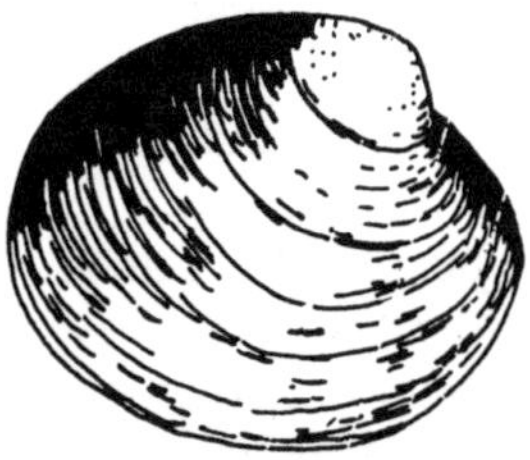

Mussels are steamed not only to cook them but to facilitate the opening of the shell.

Mussels in Cream

2 cups dry white wine
1/2 cups shallots or the white part of scallions, finely chopped
8 sprigs parsley
1 bay leaf
1/4 teaspoon thyme
pinch finely ground pepper
4 dozen mussels, scrubbed and debearded
1 cup heavy cream or half and half
1 Tablespoon arrowroot for thickening (may be omitted)

>In a large saucepan, boil the wine, shallots, herbs and pepper. Add mussels and cover tightly. Cook until shells open, about 5 minutes. When shells have opened, place the mussels in a large serving bowl and keep warm.

>Strain the cooking liquid through a fine cloth and stir in the cream blended with arrowroot. Cook over high heat three minutes more.

>Ladle the sauce over the mussels. Top with minced parsley and serve immediately.

Barbecued Hen Menu
Barbecued Cornish Game Hens
Corn on the Cob
Sautéed Vegetable Medley 147.
Green Salad
Favorite Cheesecake - page 156.

Barbecued Cornish Game Hens

My father, because he was both an actor and an olympic athlete, was seen as an authority on health and fitness. He once did an exercise book that included much of his advice and experience on keeping fit. When the book came, my siblings and I looked through it to see what dad was up to now. We found the publisher had included a recipe for "Buster Crabbe's Famous Barbecue Chicken," even though dad, to the best of our knowledge, did not enjoy barbecuing. When asked about it, he agreed that barbecue was not his forté, but added that if he did barbecue, he would like his chicken done this way. I present this recipe in his honor. I miss him.

4 game hens
1/2 teaspoon salt
7 slices bacon
2/3 cup minced onion
1/3 pound chopped chicken livers
1/2 cup butter. melted
4 slices of homestyle bread processed into crumbs
1/2 teaspoon sage
1/4 teaspoon pepper

If you do not have a covered kettle type barbecue, you can roast these in a 375° oven for about the same amount of time.
-Susan

This recipe is also good for Squab, dove, or any small game bird. The stuffing may not fit into a smaller bird, so you may have to cook it alongside the bird on the grill or in the oven. Don't forget to adjust your cooking time to compensate for the bird's size.
- Susan

Corn on the Cob is great roasted in the oven, rather than boiling it. Just butter each piece and cover it with foil, then roast at 350° for about 15 - 20 minutes. It retains more of the vitamins and flavor when prepared this way.

Beets may also be prepared in the same manner, but will require an hour to cook.

As a side dish, onions are also good this way. Peel the onion and make an X on the top and bottom with a knife so that the onion does not rupture. Wrap in foil and cook for 45 minutes at 350°. You will get the best flavor with a sweet onion such as Walla Walla or Vidalia.

-Susan

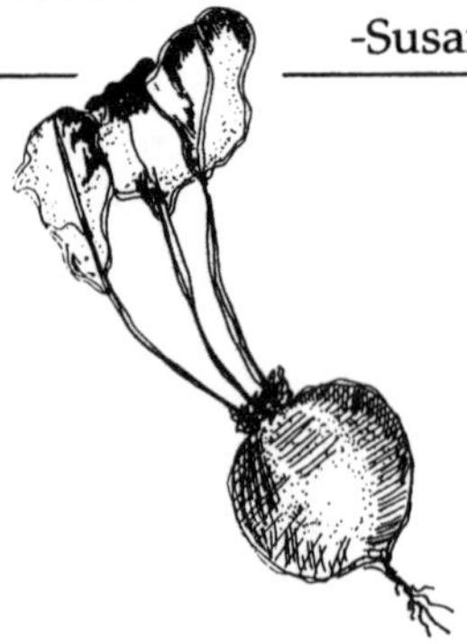

>Begin heating the charcoal to a grey red. While it is heating, prepare the game hens.
>Clean and dry hens. Sprinkle salt into the cavity of each hen.
>Dice 3 slices of bacon and cook them with the onion and liver in 1/4 cup butter until the onion is tender and the livers lose their color.
>Add bread crumbs, 1/2 teaspoon salt, sage and pepper. Stir until well blended.
>Stuff hens with the mixture and sew or skewer openings closed. Wrap a slice of bacon around each breast and secure with a wooden toothpick. Brush with remaining 1/4 cup of butter.
>After the coals begin to glow, put a drip pan made of foil under the middle of the grill on the coals to catch the grease.. Replace the grill and put the birds over the drip pan in a circle, leaving the center of the grill open.
>Cook about 45 - 60 minutes covered or until brown and well done.

Salad

We always have our salad in the European manner, after the main course. I am not totally sure why. Perhaps we felt a longing for Europe one evening, or more likely I forgot to wash the lettuce and dinner was ready. Whatever the reason, it seems to wind the dinner down. It gives us and our guests a respite during the festive atmosphere of a meal and a chance to gear up for dessert.

I like to use a mixture of different greens in my salads; salad bowl lettuce, endive, sprouts, butter lettuce, all in combination. I do not have a set proportion, just whatever looks good at the market. We add sliced tomatoes, mushrooms, radishes, celery, carrots, sometimes a crumbling of goat's cheese.

I also dress the salad lightly, in the bowl, before serving. One of my pet peeves is a salad loaded with strong dressing. A good salad does not need all that.

This is a recipe for one of my favorite homemade dressings. It can be stored in the refrigerator if you do not use it all. Always be sure to taste every dressing you make to be certain you have not added too much vinegar.

Caper Dressing

1 Tablespoon capers
1 heaping teaspoon dijon mustard
pinch salt
pinch sugar
1/2 teaspoon thyme or oregano
4 Tablespoons Balsamic vinegar
3/4 cup olive oil or salad oil

>Mix all ingredients thoroughly in blender.

To make colorful onion rings for garnishing salads, let the rings soak with pickled beets or beet juice. Walnuts or pecans toasted in butter and garlic salt are also a delicious garnish for a salad.

Use salad dressing sparingly; a thin coating is all that is needed.

The proportions for a perfect oil and vinegar dressing are one part vinegar to two parts oil.

When replacing dried herbs with fresh herbs as a general rule use twice the amount. Most fresh herbs will keep well for a few days in the refrigerator if stored in a screw top jar.

Lasagne Dinner Menu
Lasagne Rolls or White Lasagne
Marinated Vegetables
Sourdough French Bread - page 56.
Luscious Lemon Dessert - page 170.

This recipe serves a lot of people. I make this dish when preparing a party for teenagers or taking food to a pot-luck.

-Susan

When serving a meal that contains fat, plan on a citrus fruit dessert. The fruit cuts the grease and cleanses the palate.

-Susan

Lasagne Rolls

Tomato Béchamel Sauce with Herbs

1/4 cup butter
1/4 cup flour
3 Tablespoons chopped fresh basil *<u>or</u>*
1 Tablespoon dried basil
3/4 teaspoon of fresh thyme *<u>or</u>*
1/2 teaspoon dried thyme
generous pinch oregano
2 cups milk
1 cup tomato purée
3 egg yolks
salt and pepper to taste
freshly grated nutmeg
1 Tablespoon butter

>Melt butter in heavy non-aluminum sauce - pan over low heat until bubbly. Remove from heat and whisk in flour and herbs. Return to heat and cook, stirring constantly for four minutes, being certain that the flour does not brown.

>Whisk in milk and continue cooking until thickened.

>Stir in tomato purée. Remove from heat and cool for five minutes.

>Whisk in egg yolks. Season with salt, pepper and nutmeg.

>Transfer to storage container and plop 1 Tablespoon butter over the top of the sauce and allow it to melt to keep a skin from forming.
>Cover and refrigerate until ready to use.

Lasagne

1/4 cup butter
2 medium onions, finely chopped
3 cloves of garlic, minced
1/2 cup chopped almonds or pinenuts
3 pounds fresh spinach, washed and trimmed
1/3 cup raisins
1 pound ricotta cheese, drained
1/2 pound minced Italian salami, may be omitted
4 scallions, minced
1 egg yolk
3 Tablespoons parsley, minced
3 Tablespoons fresh basil or 1 Tablespoon dried
5 ounces fontinella cheese, shredded
8 ounces Parmesan cheese, grated
3 ounces Swiss or Gruyère chesse, shredded
3/4 pound lasagne noodles

>Cook spinach just until wilted, then squeeze dry and chop.
>Cook lasagne noodles according to package directions until *al dente,* then rinse in cool water, drain and pat dry with paper towels.
>Melt butter in large non-aluminum sauce pan. Add onion and cook on low heat, stirring frequently until browned and carmelized, about 25 minutes.
>Add garlic and nuts and cook 1 minute longer.
>Stir in spinach and cook until until dry.
>Remove from heat and season with salt, pepper and nutmeg. Blend in raisins and

5 packages of frozen spinach may be used in this recipe if fresh spinach is unavailable. Thaw the spinach,chop it finely, then squeeze it dry.
- Susan

When cooking pastas be sure to add a little oil to the water. Pastas have a tendency to stick together. If you want to prepare it ahead, when cooked *al dente,* remove from heat and rinse until cool. Drain and cover with a wet cloth to keep the top from drying out. To reheat, put pasta in a collander and dip into boiling water. Individual servings or the entire batch can be heated and served at your convenience.

Add pasta to the pot in handfuls, so the water doesn't fall below a boil.

As for butter vs. margarine, I trust cows more than chemists.
-Joan Gussow

let cool.
>Combine ricotta, salami, scallions, egg yolk, parsley, basil, salt and pepper in a bowl and blend.
>In another bowl blend cheeses together.
>Preheat oven to 375°. Butter a 9 inch X 13 inch baking dish and spread a thin layer of the béchamel sauce over the bottom. Whisk the sauce a few times to lighten it before putting it in the bottom of the pan .
>Lay each lasagne noodle out and spread with a thin layer of spinach and ricotta mixture. Roll up jelly roll fashion and set upright in the bottom of the pan.
>Sprinkle with the cheese mixture and pour béchamel sauce over it just before baking.
>Bake 45 to 60 minutes until bubbly and browned. Let cool slightly before serving.
Serves 10.

White Lasagne

Sauce:

3/4 cup butter
7 1/2 Tablespoons flour
2 cups milk
1 1/2 cups cream
1 cup chicken broth (reserved from the recipe below)
dash nutmeg
1/2 teaspoon rosemary, crushed
1/2 teaspoon tarragon
1/2 teaspoon Beau Monde
1 1/2 cup Parmesan cheese

3 chicken breasts, halved

1 1/4 cups chicken broth
3 quarts water
1/4 pound proscuitto ham, sliced and chopped
3 sheets fresh lasagna noodles (or 9 dry strips)

> Preheat oven to 350°.
> Poach chicken in broth and water for 1/2 hour. Reserve 1 cup broth for the sauce.
> Cut chicken into bite size pieces and set aside.
> Melt butter in a large saucepan over medium heat for 3 minutes. Add sauce liquids and stir until they boil and thicken. Add seasonings.
> Remove from heat. Add cheese.
> Lightly butter 9 inch x 13 inch pan. Layer in the following order; noodles, sauce, chicken, proscuitto. Repeat at least once, ending with noodles and sauce on the top.
> Bake at 350° for 40 minutes or until bubbly.

Marinated Vegetables

carrots
zucchini
broccoli
mushrooms
caper dressing (recipe on page 129)

>Wash all vegetables thoroughly.
>Peel carrots and cut into similar size sticks. Steam or boil until barely tender.
>Separate broccoli into florets and steam or boil until barely tender.
>Cut unpeeled zuchini into sticks and steam or boil until barely tender.
>Slice mushrooms.

A mushroom has no apparent leaves, blossoms or fruits. Indeed it is not a true plant, but a fungus. The mushroom itself is the fruit of the fungus and contains the spores or seeds. Mushrooms are very low in calories. Use mushrooms as soon as possible after buying them. Do not leave them exposed to sun or air. Mushrooms should be stored in the refrigerator in paper bags to keep them from weeping. Removing the skins weakens the structure of the mushroom, so they are best served unpeeled. When sautéing fresh mushrooms, sprinkle with a little lemon juice to prevent discoloration.

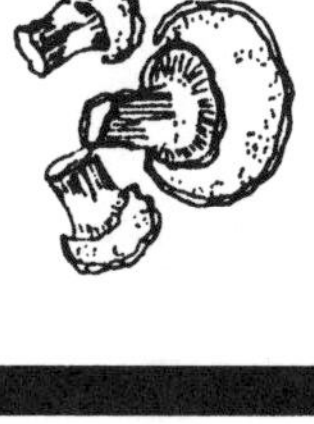

> Refrigerate each vegetable separately in a little dressing.
> At serving time arrange the vegetables on a bed of lettuce, alternating them around the plate and piling the mushrooms in the center. Cover with remaining dressing.

Dinner at the Inn

Mushroom Soup, page 80.
Gourges, page 90.
Butterflied Leg of Lamb with Peanut Sauce
Simple Wild Rice
Purée of Squash, page 123.
Homemade French Bread, page 56.
Salad of Fresh Seasonal Greens, Sliced Mushrooms, Fresh Tomatoes, Radishes and Chevre
Warm Chocolate-Espresso Pudding Cakes, page 160.

Internal Temperature Guide

Beef - 140° rare
160° medium
170° well done
Lamb - 175° medium
180° well done
Veal - 170° well done

A rack of lamb is usually seven ribs. One rack will feed 2 to 3 people, depending on their appetite.

Butterflied Leg of Lamb with Peanut Sauce

This sauce is also tasty with chicken. Please note that the lamb must be marinated ahead of time.

Peanut Sauce:

2 Tablespoons peanut oil
1 small onion, minced
2 cloves garlic, peeled and minced
1 Tablespoon brown sugar
1/2 teaspoon crushed red pepper
1 cup chicken stock
1 cup chunky peanut butter

1 drop tabasco
2 teaspoons soy sauce
2 Tablespoons lemon juice

> Sauté onion and garlic in oil in a skillet until soft and translucent but do not let brown.
> Add brown sugar and red pepper. Cook over low heat while stirring for a couple of minutes.
> Add stock, peanut butter and the drop of tabasco. Cook, stirring constantly until smoothly blended.
> Remove from heat and add soy sauce and lemon juice. Add additional stock or water if too thick.

---

1 leg of lamb, boned
1/2 cup lemon juice
1/3 cup brown sugar
3 Tablespoons Dijon Mustard
1/4 cup soy sauce
1/2 cup olive oil
3 cloves garlic, peeled and minced
1/2 teaspoon freshly ground pepper
1/2 inch piece of fresh ginger, peeled and sliced

> Mix all ingredients together and marinade meat in mixture. Marinade at least three hour or up to overnight in the refrigerator.
> Grill lamb on barbecue, skin side down for 15 minutes. Turn and finish cooking, cut side down, about 10 minutes more. Meat should be pink inside.
> Serve with Peanut Sauce.

Mary had a little lamb,
You've heard this tale before;
But did you know
She passed her plate
And had a little more?
- Folk Rhyme

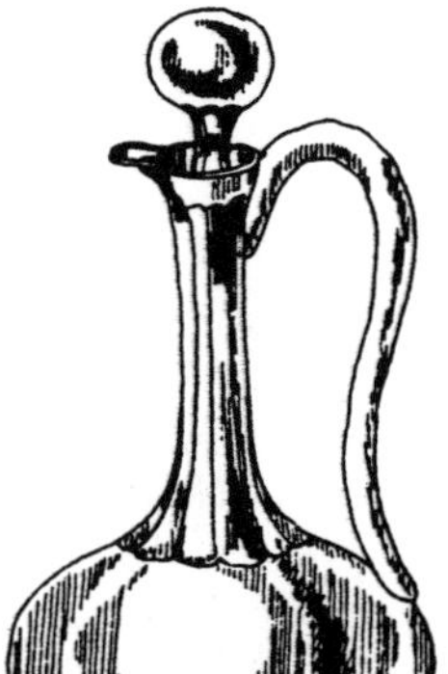

When serving buffet style, stack large dinner plates at the start of the line and napkins and silverware at the other end. This frees up hands to fill plates.

It's a funny thing about life. If you refuse to accept anything but the best, you very often get it.

-W. Somerset Maugham

Simple Wild Rice

My favorite side dish for birds of all kinds.

1 cup wild rice
1/2 cup chopped walnuts
1 1/2 Tablespoons butter

> Cook rice according to package directions.
> Toast walnuts in a skillet with the butter.
> Mix rice and walnuts. Season to taste.

Pork Medallions

This is a great dish for the grill. The Spiced Applesauce recipe on page 144 is a fantastic accompaniment, but should be made ahead and chilled.

Marinade:

1/4 cup soy sauce
2 Tablespoons Dijon mustard
1/2 cup dry sherry
2 garlic cloves, peeled and minced
2 Tablespoons grated fresh ginger root
1/2 teaspoon fresh thyme
1/2 teaspoon black pepper

8 boneless medallions of pork
3 Tablespoons fresh lemon juice
1/2 cup mint jelly
2 Tablespoons sherry
2 Tablespoons soy sauce

>Combine the marinade ingredients in a nonreactive baking dish. Marinade the pork chops for 1/2 hour, turning once or twice.
> Drain the chops, reserving the marinade. Grill or broil the chops to the desired degree of doneness (this will depend on thickness), basting occasionally. Set the chops aside and keep warm.
> Place the remaining marinade in a sauce pan and bring to a boil over high heat. Boil until the sauce is reduced to 4 Tablespoons, about 5 minutes.
> Stir in the sherry, lemon juice, soy sauce and mint jelly. Heat through and pour over pork chops.
>Serve with Spiced Applesauce.

Use of Herbs

Herbs have a long history and have been used for dyes, repelling insects, and curing illness, as well as adding flavor to foods. When buying or using dried herbs be cautious, they lose flavor rapidly when exposed to light, air, or heat. When in doubt, sniff. Herbs were also known as the symbol of certain characteristics. Below is a small sample:

Basil - royalty
Rosemary - remembrance and friendship
Sage - wisdom
Borage - bravery
Comfrey - purity

Countries and Their Cheeses

Sweden - Mesost, Sveciaost
Dutch - Gouda, Edam
Greek - Feta, Graviera
England - Stilton
French - Roquefort
U.S.A. - Cheddar, Jack
Italian -Mozarella, Ricotta Parmesan

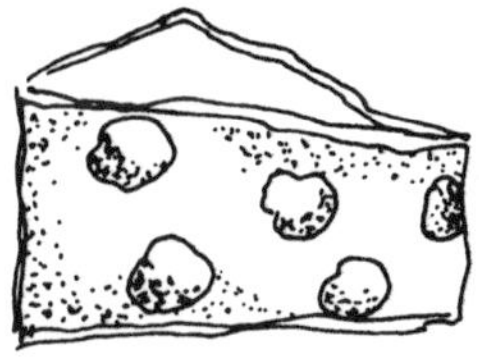

A warm smile is the universal language of kindness.
- Wm. Arthur Ward

Pacific Rim Mussels

3 Tablespoons olive oil
1/2 teaspoon sesame oil
1/2 cup thinly sliced scallions
1 teaspoon finely chopped or minced shallots
1 Tablespoon fresh minced ginger
1 teaspoon curry powder
1 teaspoon chili powder
1/4 teaspoon cayenne pepper
1 can (14 ounces) unsweetened coconut milk
2 to 2 1/2 dozen mussels (we use either Penn Cove or Lopez Island)
1 cup dry white wine
2 Tablespoons chopped parsley
3 Tablespoons chopped fresh basil

> Put the sesame oil and olive oil in a large pot with a tight fitting lid. Add the scallions, shallots and ginger to the oils and gently heat and soften.

> Add seasoning and wine to the pot and bring to a boil. Add mussels and cook uncovered until the shells open (about 5-7 minutes). As soon as the shells open, add coconut milk, chopped parsley and basil.

> Spoon into the bowl and serve with crusty bread.

Mussels in a Minute

3 pounds mussels, debearded and scrubbed
3/4 cup water
3/4 cup dry white wine
1 Tablespoon butter
1 Tablespoon olive oil
1/2 cup chopped onion
2 cloves garlic, crushed
3 Tablespoons chopped parsley

> In a large pot with a tightly fitting lid, soften onion, garlic and parsley in butter and oil. When just colored, add water and wine and bring to a boil.
> Add mussels, cover and steam until mussels are wide opened and fully cooked.
> Serve with crusty french bread, a big green salad and a cool glass of Chardonnay for a very simple but satisfying meal.
> Serves 4.

To clarify butter:
Melt two Tablespoons butter in a small heavy saucepan over low heat until butter melts and white sediment gathers on the bottom of the pan. Pour off clear yellow liquid. Discard sediment. Refrigerate clarified butter and use as needed.

Fish Cakes

At a recent annual meeting of The Independent Innkeepers Association, held at the Red Lion Inn in Stockbridge, Massachusetts, we had the pleasure of attending a lavish buffet at Blantyre. Blantyre is a fabulous property owned by the Fitzpatrick family, who also owns the Red Lion. One of my favorite dishes that evening was their Cod Fish cakes (if you can imagine such a simple dish rising to the forefront amidst such plenty). I played around with the ingredients that I suspected

Basic Sauces
Bearnaise - butter, wine, tarragon
Hollandaise - egg yolks, butter, lemon juice
Béchamel - basic white sauce
Mornay - white sauce with cheese
Remoulade - egg yolk, mustard, lemon juice, spices
Beurre Noir - black butter, wine, lemon juice
Beurre Blanc - cream, butter, lemon juice, Vermouth

were in these cakes and I humbly offer the following.

---

2 pounds cod fillets, such as ling cod, cut into 2 inch pieces
1 onion, finely chopped
2 ribs celery, finely chopped
2 large sliced mushrooms
2 Tablespoons butter
2 Tablespoons parsley, chopped
2 teaspoons grated lemon zest
1 Tablespoon lemon juice
1 teaspoon seasoned salt, such as Old Bay Seasoning, or to taste
1/2 teaspoon pepper
yellow cornmeal
2 Tablespoons oil for frying

> Sauté onions, celery, and mushrooms in 1 Tablespoon butter until softened.
> In a food processor, purée fish until light and smooth. Add onions, celery and mushrooms, parsley, lemon zest and lemon juice, salt and pepper. Pulse until well blended.
> Wet hands and shape into 8 round patties. Dust patties with cornmeal.
> In a large skillet melt 1 Tablespoon butter with 2 Tablespoons oil. Sauté cakes over medium, high heat, turning once until nicely browned on the outside and cooked through.
> Drain on a paper towel, if necessary, and serve with spicy tarter sauce.

Spicy Tarter Sauce

1 cup mayonnaise, preferably homemade
1 Tablespoon capers
1 Tablespoon finely chopped cornichon pickles
1 1/2 teaspoons Dijon mustard
1 teaspoon lemon juice

> Mix the above ingredients at least 1 hour before serving to allow flavors to blend.

Chicken Country Captain

This is my mother's recipe. I have different versions in various cookbooks, but I still like her version the best.

3 fryers or 12 chicken breasts
3 green peppers, quartered, seeded, and sliced
3 - #2 cans solid packed tomatoes
1/2 cup chopped parsley
3 medium onions, chopped
2 cloves garlic, minced
1 teaspoon salt
1/2 teaspoon thyme
1 teaspoon curry powder
1/2 teaspoon black pepper, freshly ground
1/2 pound blanched almonds, toasted and slivered
1 cup currants
1 cup shredded coconut, unsweetened
1 cup flour, mixed with 1/2 teaspoon paprika, and salt and pepper to taste
2 Tablespoons butter
2 Tablespoons olive oil

The Chicken Chart

Broilers - The smallest of chickens at 1 to 2 ½ pounds, broilers are young chickens with very little fat.

Broilers/Fryers - At 2 ½ to 4 ½ pounds, butchers use the terms interchangeably. These birds can be prepared either way. Look for yellow fat and plump breasts.

Roasters/Pullets - At 3 ½ to 7 ½ pounds, these birds are tender and meaty. They are good for barbecuing, roasting, or baking.

Capons - Castrated when young, these 10 week old cocks weigh between 8 to 10 pounds. Their meat is delicate and tender with an abundance of white meat.

Hens and Fowl - These are the most flavorful birds, but can be the toughest at 10 months or older. Weighing 3 to 8 pounds, they require longer and slower cooking.

Tips for shucking an oyster:

- Briefly rinse shells under running water.
- Put on a heavy glove and grab a clean hand towel.
- Grasp the shell with the hinged end uncovered and cup side in the palm of your hand to retain as much liquid as possible.
- Rinse the oyster knife between shellings.
- Twist, do not pry at the hinge. Some oysters have very delicate shells and will crack in half if forcibly pried.

Crackers and bread slices are not the only means of holding dips. Cucumber slices, endive or spinach leaves, apple or pear slices, and zucchini wedges make good cracker substitutes.

- Susan

> Preheat oven to 350°.
> Cut chicken into serving pieces and roll pieces in flour mixture.
> Lightly brown the pieces in butter and oil.
> Put chicken in a large roasting pan and add 1/2 cup water.
> In the pan the chicken was browned in, add pepper, onion, and garlic. Cook until they begin to brown, being careful not to burn either the garlic or onion. When slightly browned, add thyme, curry powder, parsley, salt, pepper, tomatoes and 1/2 cup water. Cook for 15 minutes.
> Pour mixture over chicken, cover and bake one hour, or until chicken is tender.
> Serve over wild, brown, or white rice. Garnish each plate with a sprinkle of coconut, currants, and slivered almonds.

Serves 6.

Carpetbag Steak for the Barbecue

This recipe as well as the oyster one that follows was given to me by Char Bawden, who owns Judd Cove Oysters.

4 filet mignon steaks, about 6 ounces each
8 small Judd Cove oysters
1/4 cup softened butter
2 garlic cloves, crushed
2 Tablespoons finely chopped parsley
Fresh ground pepper to taste

> Using a sharp knife, slit each filet lengthwise to form a packet.
> Shuck the oysters. In a bowl, mix the

oysters, butter, garlic and parsley. Add pepper to taste.
> Place equal amounts of oyster mixture in the steak packets. Close with a toothpick or small skewer.
> Cook each steak on the grill to individual taste, roughly 5 - 8 minutes.

Serves 4.

Oysters Bubbly

This is a fun summer appetizer.

1 small onion, minced
4 Tablespoons butter
1 cup brut champagne
1/2 teaspoon salt
1/2 teaspoon white pepper, fresh ground
16 - 20 Judd Cove oysters, shucked but reserving their liquor
2 Tablespoons flour
2 Tablespoons heavy cream
lemon wedges

> In a large saucepan over medium heat, cook onions in 2 Tablespoons butter until softened, about 2 minutes.
> Pour in champagne, add salt and pepper. Reduce heat to low.
> Add oysters and the reserved liquor. Cover and simmer until oysters are slightly firm, about 2 minutes.
> In a small bowl, combine 2 Tablespoons butter and flour, work mixture into a smooth paste.
> Add pea size amounts of flour to cham-

Refrigerate unopened oysters in a baking dish with a damp towel laid over them. Do not put oysters in water or in a container with a tight fitting plastic lid. They need to breathe.

Judd Cove Oysters have such a sweet, delicate flavor that they are delicious raw and unadorned. They are also great off the grill. Here are a couple of tips for grilling them.
- Place oysters cup side down to retain liquor while cooking.
- Keep on the grill until the liquor starts to bubble around the edge and shells open slightly.

If you refrigerate candles for several hours before using them, you will have less drips.

Best Oils for Health
Olive Oil
Canola Oil
Almond Oil

Garlic is a vegetable. It is a member of the lily family, which includes onions, leeks, scallions, and shallots.

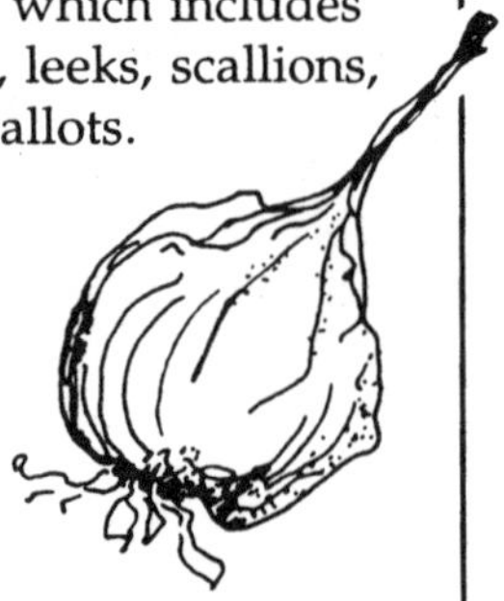

pagne and oysters. Stir constantly until all the flour is mixed in and the sauce thickens.
> Stir in cream and cook one minute longer.
> Serve in individual ramekins with lemon wedges as garnish.

Spiced Applesauce

Pippin, Northern Spy and Jonagold apples grow in the orchard at Turtleback. They are my favorite choices for this dish.

6 to 8 medium apples, unpeeled
Sugar to taste
2 Tablespoons fresh lemon juice
3 Tablespoons prepared horseradish

>Wash, quarter, and core the apples.
> Place them in a saucepan and partially cover with water. Simmer until the apples are tender, about 20 minutes.
>Purée apples in a ricer or food processor, skin and all.
> Sweeten to taste with sugar and return to the saucepan. Cook for three more minutes.
> Stir in the horseradishand lemon, and chill for at least 30 minutes.

Serves 4.

Baked Winter Fruits

Spiced with candied ginger, allspice, and cinnamon, this flavorful dish can be served with yogurt for breakfast or as an accompaniment to pork or game.

1 pound dried apricots, halved
1 pound dried peaches, coarsely chopped
4 Tablespoons (1/2 stick) unsalted butter
1 1/4 cups dry white wine
1 cup firmly packed dark brown sugar
1 teaspoon minced candied ginger
1 teaspoon vanilla extract
grated zest and juice of 1 lemon
1/4 teaspoon ground cinnamon
1/4 teaspoon ground allspice
1/4 teaspoon ground ginger
1 cup chopped walnuts

> Butter a 2-quart glass baking dish. Mix the dried fruits together.
> Place half of the fruit in the bottom of the prepared dish and dot with 2 Tablespoons of the butter cut into small bits. Spread the remaining fruit on top and dot with the remaining 2 Tablespoons of butter.
> Combine the wine, sugar, ginger, vanilla, lemon zest and juice, and spices. Blend thoroughly and pour over the fruit.
> Sprinkle with walnuts and cover with foil. Refrigerate overnight.
> One hour before baking, remove the fruit from the refrigerator.
>Preheat the over to 375°.
> Bake the fruit, covered, for about 45 minutes, or until it has plumped and the liquid has become caramelized.

For fast-acting relief, try slowing down.
- Lily Tomlin

White meat cooks more quickly than dark meat.

A fanatic is one who can't change his mind, and won't change the subject.
- Sir Winston Churchill

> Uncover and cool. Serve at room temperature. Serves 8.

Caramelized Onions with Fresh Ginger

This onion side dish was prepared for us one evening as we shared dinner with Perla Meyers and her family. Perla Meyers is an award-winning author of five cookbooks. She contributes articles and recipes to many publications and is an internationally known chef and teacher. She, her husband and her son visited Orcas and Turtleback Farm a couple of years ago. We served squab (young pigeons) Bill raises here. This onion dish was a perfect compliment to this meal and goes well with any hearty dinner.

4 Tablespoons olive oil
5 or 6 large onions, peeled, quartered and thinly sliced
2 large cloves of garlic, peeled and thinly sliced
1 Tablespoon sugar
3 Tablespoons (heaping) fresh ginger, minced
2 Tablespoons balsamic vinegar

> Heat the oil in a large, heavy skillet.
> Add the onions and garlic. Sprinkle with sugar and cook over low to moderate heat.
> After about five minutes, add ginger and vinegar to onions and continue cooking, stirring often until the onions soften and brown. This will take at least 30 minutes.

Be careful to keep the heat low enough that the onions do not burn. They will become caramelized with a lovely brown color.

Sautéed Vegetable Medley

If you refrigerate onions before you slice or chop them, they will not bring tears to your eyes.

1 large onion, thinly sliced
4 Tablespoons olive oil
2 cloves garlic, minced
1 eggplant, cut into cubes, salted and left to stand in colander
1 zucchini, thinly sliced
1 yellow squash, thinly sliced
1 green pepper, cored, seeded, sliced into strips
1 red pepper, cored, seeded and sliced into strips
1 large tomato, diced
1/2 cup white wine
1 teaspoon basil
1 teaspoon oregano
salt and freshly ground pepper to taste

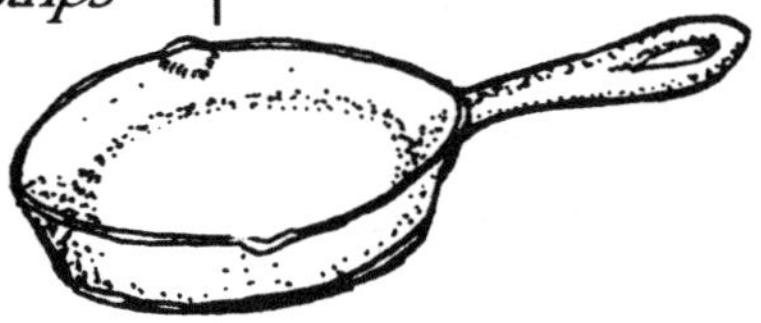

> In a large skillet, sauté onion in oil over medium heat until golden.
> Turn down the heat, add garlic and cook a bit more, being careful not to scorch.
> Add eggplant, coating well with the oil in the pan. If there isn't much oil remaining, add a bit more.
> Cook, stirring often, for about 5 minutes, then add peppers and tomatoes. Stir and cover.
> Cook until eggplant becomes soft, checking often so the mixture doesn't dry out. If it seems dry, add 1/2 cup white wine.
> When the eggplant is soft, add squash and cook until they are done.
> This can be served with a sprinkle of parmesan cheese and is good the next day.

Carrots are most flavorful if you do not add salt to them while they are cooking. Add a small bit of sugar instead.

A bowl of fresh herbs by the front door makes a welcoming aroma for your guests.

I think of life as a good book. The further you get into it, the more it begins to make sense.
- Harold S. Kushner

Fun Garnish for Dinner Plates

Citrus Butterflies

Choose a firm piece of citrus fruit (lemon, lime or orange) that has few seeds. Take a very sharp knife and cut into thin slices. Remove the seeds. Cut a V shaped wedge from the slice. Turn the slice around and cut another wedge making this one larger than the first. Discard the cutout pieces. You should have two triangular shaped pieces, thinly attatched. Place two thin strips of red bell pepper to represent the feelers.

Washington Wines

In a very short span of years, Washington State has quietly asserted itself as the most important wine growing district in the United States outside of California. With only a fraction of the acreage that California has devoted to grape culture, and a very different set of circumstances to cope with climatically, modern pioneers of the Washington wine industry have in the last quarter century found ways to overcome limiting factors, such as temperature.

Over the centuries of wine growing, it has been observed that vines of greatest character are the offspring of vines rooted in poor, well drained soils relatively low in humus content. These soils are normally not favorable to crop production. In the middle of the last century, plant material shipped from North America to Europe delivered an unexpected plague to European vineyards, a root louse known as phylloxera. By the late 1800's, phylloxera had practically wiped out all vineyard plantings in Europe, causing a wine crisis and establishing a need to find a solution for future pest resistant healthy vineyards. The solution finally arrived upon was to graft the European vine types on hybrid North American rootstock. This practice has successfully reestablished vineyards in Europe, and allowed for the development of wine growing districts in North America.

This story becomes important to Washington vintners because of the very cold and prolonged winter temperatures to which their vines are exposed. It was discovered that vines planted deeply on their own roots could recover true to type from a winter kill to ground level. Phylloxen has not become a problem, perhaps because of poor sandy soils or harsh winter temperatures. One has to wonder if this gives Washington wines a character more akin to their ancestors than the grafted vines prevalent today.

East Washington's northern latitude combined with its

desert dry conditions, soils, and cool night temperatures, allow grapes to ripen fully while retaining their natural acidity. This acidity is the key to the brilliance and freshness of Washington wines.

The primary limiting factors for Washington wines are lack of water and long cold winters with occasional prolonged temperatures below 0°. The solution to the lack of water is drip irrigation systems. Vintners also discovered that planting primarily on southern sloping exposures would give plantings the benefit of sun and cold air drainage below vineyard elevation. This practice, in addition to planting vines on their own roots so they would return to ground true to variety next season, dramatically reduced lost production time to only one year.

In today's dynamic arena, some of the most important producers of fine wine are the following:

Andrew Will - Cabernet Sauvignon/Merlot
Barnard Griffin - Fumé Blanc/Chardonnay/Merlot
Canoe Ridge Winery - Chardonnay/ Merlot
Chinook Winery - Chardonnay/Sauvignon Blanc/ Semillon/Merlot
Columbia Winery - vineyard designated Cabernet Sauvignon
Columbia Crest - Chardonnay/Merlot/Cabernet Sauvignon
Hogue Cellars - Riesling/Sauvignon Blanc/Semillon/Merlot
Leonetti Cellars - Merlot/ Cabernet Sauvignon
L'Ecole No. 41 - Semillon/Chardonnay/Merlot/ Cabernet Sauvignon
Ste. Michelle - Riesling/Chardonnay/Cabernet Sauvignon
Quilceda Creek - Cabernet Sauvignon
Waterbrook Winery - Chardonnay/ Cabernet Sauvignon
Woodward Canyon Winery - Chardonnay/Merlot / Cabernet Sauvignon

A Guide to Wines

Chardonnay - A thick textured white wine with green apple and sometimes tropical pineapple and coconut flavors, Chardonnays are often described as buttery or creamy. Excellent with white meats: chicken, pork, and some seafood, especially when the wine is not heavily influenced by oak.

Sauvignon Blanc - Sometimes referred to as Fumé Blanc, this wine is crisp, clean, and refreshing with a distinctive piercing aroma sometimes described as grassy or herbaceous. An exceptional companion to seafood, particularly sweet shellfish such as crab, lobster, scallops and oysters. Also pairs well with some cheese, especially those made from goat's milk.

Semillon - Historically these grapes were blended with Sauvignon Blanc to produce the great dry and sweet wines of Bordeaux. However, this white grape has produced some very interesting dry wines in Washington with a bit more fat on the palate than Sauvignon Blanc, but pretty melon flavors and refreshing acidity. Pairs well with seafood, especially oysters.

Riesling - This grape produces an intense floral and mineral flavor and aroma with viscous palate and crispy acidity. It adapts well to dry or late harvest dessert styles. Serve with freshwater fish, white meats, fruits and cheese or at meals end, depending on style.

Cabernet Sauvignon - This is a red wine of power and structure, exhibiting cedar and black currant fruit. The potential is there for improvement with bottle age. Classically paired with beef, lamb, duck, game, and cheese.

Merlot - Currently the darling of wine consumers and media, this plum and cherry pie fruit is often married with tasty oak to yield a wine of irresistible lushness. There are usually less of the firm tannin associated with a Cabernet Sauvignon. Food affinities are similar to Cabernet, but try it with salmon and fowl.

John Trumbull of Rose's Bread and Specialties in Eastsound Square contributed the information on Washington Wines.

All of us have different ideas about what is necessary for good health. For those of us who earn our living in the city, just getting away from our daily work environment can be the first step toward restoring our health and sanity. For those who live in rural areas, a trip to the city might be needed to shake off the effects of cabin fever. We have devoted this chapter to what we feel is a basic component of good health, both physical and mental, the sweets of the palate and the sweets of the soul.

Health experts tell us the most helpful aspect of a vacation is the exposure to different sensory input. Our minds and bodies need pleasant new experiences from time to time to keep us alert, healthy and happy. We believe this so much that we do not use the term vacation when we travel. This word implies to vacate the mind, which is what many of us do in our daily routines, where mindfulness often is not a requirement. Instead we prefer the word holiday. If we do it right, a trip, or even a good meal, is a holiday; a filling of the senses with sounds, tastes, sights, textures, celebration and new perspectives.

There are many ways to take holidays, some big and some small. Travel forces us to discover dormant talents and abilities because we can not fall back on the familiar in strange environments. Orcas Island brought our health to mind because the island has a reputation for being a place of rejuvenation. Testament to the true nature of Orcas is the Healing Arts Center, almost in the center of the island. There one can receive or learn to give a massage, among other therapeutic possibilities.

Probably the biggest part of the healing Orcas Island offers is its rural setting. The constant stimulation of the traffic, people and noise that we find in the city is more of a jolt to the system than a soothing hand. On Orcas, there are no malls, entertainment centers or nightclubs to offer distraction. The term party is most often applied to a potluck barbecue. The locals like it that way. After all, they go to Seattle when they want an adventure. We found Orcas, like many rural destinations, a great place to unplug from the television, the news and the world in general and wrap ourselves in a cocoon of fresh experiences.

But one need not travel to an island to have this experience. There are ways to create this experience in our everyday environment, the most obvious being keeping a promise to ourselves to try new things. This is one reason that we believe in mini-holidays. We have found that when we have the blahs, just going to a new restaurant, or putting together a new dish at home is often enough to pull us out of it. A little new stimulation is sometimes all the body and mind needs to feel the enjoyment of life once again. This can be a new dance step, a walk in the park, a different restaurant or a new recipe. Wherever you live, we recommend you take the time to get away from it all from time to time. Turn the television off, put on your favorite music, let the answering machine take your calls, sip a little wine, and whip up a treat in the kitchen. It will definitely make your stay on planet earth more fun and relaxing. And it might add a few years to your life.

There are sure to be those who protest, but we strongly believe that sweets and desserts are somehow connected to longevity. Desserts in themselves are not dangerous or sinful, despite what you may have been told. It is the quantity in which we eat them that can become disastrous. A health magazine to which we subscribe recently featured an article on the importance of having dessert. The article informed us how dessert can round out the nutrients in a meal, especially when the sweet contains fresh fruit. In small quantities, generally 2 to

4 tablespoons, even really rich desserts like hot fudge sundaes, can keep our sweet tooth at bay and ward off those often regretted binging sprees. Better an ounce of something wonderful, we are told, than a pound of denial and longing or a frenzy of over-indulgence. (Although a friend of mine described these portions as exquisite torture.)

But another important aspect of those special foods and events is that they keep our outlook bright. The evidence is quickly mounting that a lack of stress in our lives is not the optimum condition. Rather than a state of perpetual relaxation, we need lives rich with things we enjoy. People, places, events and foods that please us stimulate our minds and bodies, as well as make staying alive worthwhile. These benefits are strongest, we believe, when we do whatever it is that pleases us in a conscious state of mind. In other words, if you treat yourself to the delicacies of a chocolate mousse, enjoy every bite. Let all your senses take in the experience and savor it for all it's worth. As our parents taught us, anything worth doing is worth doing well. We see no reason why that maxim shouldn't be applied to desserts.

Spiced Cup Cakes

1 cup raisins
2 cups water
1/2 cup shortening
1 3/4 cups flour, sifted
1 cup sugar
1 teaspoon baking soda
pinch salt
1 teaspoon cinnamon
1 teaspoon clove
1 teaspoon allspice
1 teaspoon nutmeg
1 egg, beaten
1/2 cup or more chopped nuts

We have all been to potluck's. But have you ever considered an all dessert one? These are especially good over celebrational or holiday times. Add a couple of dessert wines and coffee and you have an instant party.

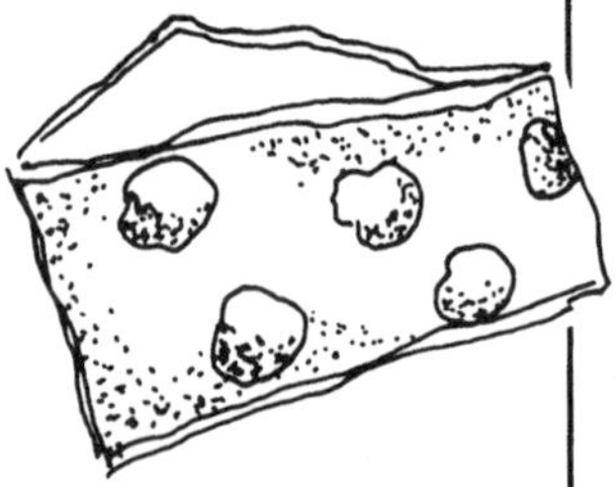

When cutting a cheesecake or any gooey dessert, run warm water over your knife first. The slices will cut cleaner.

>Boil raisins in water for 10 minutes. Let cool for 5 minutes.
>Preheat oven to 375°. Grease and flour muffin tins or line with paper liners.
>Add shortening to raisins.
>Mix dry ingredients together. Add to raisin mixture.
>Add beaten egg and nuts. Stir to blend.
>Pour into prepared muffin tins. Fill each cup a little over 1/2 full. Bake for 30-40 minutes or until done. Can be frosted with buttercream frosting or served plain.

Makes 12 cupcakes.

Favorite Cheesecake

Crust

1 package graham crackers
4 Tablespoons butter
1 1/4 Tablespoons sugar

>Preheat oven to 350°.
>Process the above in a food processor with on/off pulses until the crackers are uniform crumbs. Press into the bottom and up the sides of a 10 inch springform pan.
>Bake 10 minutes or until lightly browned. Cool.

Filling

2- 8 ounce packages cream cheese
1/2 cup sugar
2 eggs
1/2 teaspoon vanilla

>Preheat oven to 375°.
>Process all the filling ingredients in a food processor until the mixture is smooth, about 3 minutes. Scrape down the sides and process again to insure that the mixture is well blended.
>Pour into prepared crust and bake for 25 minutes. Cool 30 minutes.

Topping

2 cups sour cream
2 Tablespoons sugar
1/2 teaspoon vanilla

>Preheat oven to 475°.
>Blend together all ingredients. Cover the cream cheese mixture with the topping.
>Return to the oven and bake for 5 minutes.
>Remove from the oven. Cool, then refrigerate at least 4 hours or overnight.

Spiced Pound Cake

This is a versatile pound cake. It is good enough to serve plain or it can be dressed up with fresh fruits, sherbets or ice creams.

1 cup butter
1 1/2 teaspoon freshly grated nutmeg
1/2 teaspoon salt
1 2/3 cups sugar
5 eggs
2 cups flour

>Do not preheat oven, but have ingredients

Physical appearance is often a reflection of a person's health. No physical attribute tells more about a person's health than their skin. A nutritious diet, exercise, fresh air and lots of water will to give the skin a healthy glow. Facial masks not only deep clean the skin, but they are soothing as well. Such masks can often be made at home from natural ingredients. One of our favorites is made from crushed almonds. Add a liquid, such as milk, yogurt or water to the almond meal and make a paste. Apply this to a clean face, allow it to dry, then wash it off with cool water. Almond oil is used in making creams, lotions and body oils.

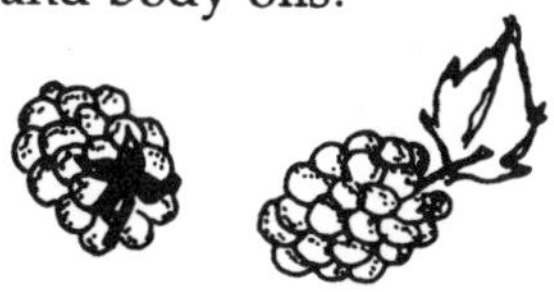

A cake will be less likely to stick to the pan if you put the pan on a wet towel to cool as soon as you remove it from the oven.

A few marigold petals added to bread dough or cake batter will give the resulting baked good a pale yellow color and a wonderful flavor. One tablespoon is generally all that is needed.

Cake flour makes a lighter cake without any sifting.
-Susan

at room temperature.
>Grease and flour tube pan.
>Beat butter, nutmeg and salt with mixer for 5 minutes. Add sugar and beat until fluffy, 2 minutes or more.
>Beat in 4 of the eggs, one at a time.
>Stir in all of the flour and beat again about 3 minutes. Beat in the last egg just until thoroughly mixed.
>Pour batter into a greased pan and place into the cold oven.
>Turn oven on to 300° and bake for 2 hours or until a cake tester comes out clean.
>Cool in pan about 10 minutes. Then turn out onto a wire rack to cool completely.

Orange Cake

1 1/4 cups flour plus 1 Tablespoon
2 teaspoons baking powder
1/4 teaspoon baking soda
peel of one orange, only the orange skin, not any of the white
1 cup sugar
3 large eggs, room temperature
1/2 cup butter, room temperature
1/2 cup fresh orange juice
glaze, (recipe follows)

>Preheat oven to 375°.
>Grease and flour a 6 1/2 cup bundt pan or ring mold.
>Mix all dry ingredients except sugar in a bowl.
>Place the orange peel in the bowl of the

food processor and chop. Add 1/2 cup sugar and process until very fine. Add the remaining sugar and eggs and process for 1 minute. Scrape the sides of the bowl and process again about 10 seconds.
>Add butter. Process for 1 minute. Scrape down the sides of the bowl and process until fluffy, about 1 minute.
>With the machine running, pour orange juice down feed tube and process until well blended.
>Add flour mixture and process until just blended, about 3-4 pulses.
>Pour batter into prepared pan and spread evenly.
>Bake 20-25 minutes or until cake pulls away from the sides of pan and a tester comes out clean. Watch carefully because this cake is easy to overbake.
>Invert on cooling rack and let cool while you prepare the glaze.

Glaze

1/4 cup apricot jam
1 Tablespoon lemon juice
1 Tablespoon sugar
1 Tablespoon rum

>Boil jam, lemon juice and sugar together until bubbly, about 2 minutes.
>Strain mixture into a bowl.
>Let cool a little and add rum.
>Slowly pour warm glaze over warm cake so the mixture is absorbed.
>Serve slices of cooled cake with the topping of your choice.

Suggested Toppings:
vanilla ice cream
whipping cream
yogurt sweetened with a little honey
apricot slices
nectarine slices
nasturtiums
borage
fruit purèes
creme fraiche
chocolate shavings
melba sauce
favorite liqueur

Pears make a wonderful dessert. Choose either Bartlett, Anjou or Bosc pears. In a pan large enough to hold 6 pears side-by-side, boil 1 3/4 cups of dry red wine,1 cup sugar, 1/4 teaspoon anise seeds, 2 cinnamon sticks and 2 lemon slices. Add pears, reduce heat to medium and simmer until Bartletts are heated and still hold their shape and the Bosc and Anjou can be pierced easily with a fork, about 12-15 minutes. Remove pears with a spoon and reduce cooking liquid to a syrup. Pour over the pears. Serve warm.

Whenever a recipe calls for granulated sugar, consider using bartender's sugar. Its fine texture lends itself well to light desserts. To make your own super fine sugar, process granulated sugar in a food processor until powdery. Make sure the processor is dry before processing.

While an original is always hard to find, he is easy to recognize.
- John L. Mason

Warm Chocolate-Espresso Pudding Cakes

3/4 cup butter or margarine
6 ounces bittersweet chocolate, chopped
4 1/2 Tablespoons unbleached white flour
2 Tablespoons unsweetened cocoa
2 teaspoons freeze dried espresso powder or 2 Tablespoons hot espresso
1/3 cup sugar
5 large eggs, separated
1 1/2 Tablespoons Kahlua
1/2 teaspoon vanilla

> Preheat oven to 375°.
> In a small pan, combine butter and chocolate. Heat over low heat until melted and smoothly mixed. Add espresso and mix.
> Mix together flour and cocoa.
> In a large bowl beat the 5 egg whites until they become white. Beat in 1 Tablespoon sugar at a time until the eggs hold stiff and shiny but not dry peaks.
> Blend together the yolks, liqueur, vanilla, and the cocoa/flour mixture, then add the chocolate/butter mixture. Gently fold in the egg whites.
> Pour about 1/2 cup batter into each of 8 buttered ramekins or custard cups.
> For ease of handling, place the ramekins on a cookie sheet before placing in the oven to bake. Bake until the edges begin to firm but the center is still soft when pressed, 11-12 minutes.
> Let cool for a few minutes, then invert onto serving plates.

Serve with coffee ice cream.

Espresso Cheesecake

2 cups crushed Oreo or chocolate wafer cookies
1/4 cup butter, melted
4 - 8 ounce packages cream cheese
3 eggs
1/2 cup sour cream
1/4 cup Kahlua
1/4 cup strong espresso
3/4 cup firmly packed brown sugar
1 teaspoon vanilla
3/4 teaspoon salt

> Preheat oven to 350°.
> Mix crushed cookies with butter. Blend thoroughly, then press into the bottom and sides of spring-form pan. Set aside.
> Blend the remaining ingredients and pour into prepared pan.
> Bake 1 hour.
> Cool completely, then chill overnight before serving.

Sour Cream Chocolate Cake

3 squares unsweetened chocolate
1/2 cup water
1 cup sour cream
1 3/4 cups unsifted flour
1 1/2 teaspoon baking powder
1 teaspoon salt
1 teaspoon soda
2/3 cup butter
2/3 cup firmly packed brown sugar
1 cup granulated sugar

Egg whites at room temperature beat up faster and to a larger volume than cold ones. A properly beaten white should triple its volume. Egg whites will not beat up properly if either the bowl or beaters are even slightly moist or greasy.

-Susan

Cheese should always be served at room temperature for the best taste and texture.

Few things are more soothing than a hot cup of herb tea. Camomile tea is a natural relaxer; tea made from rosehips contains a large amount of vitamin C; mint teas aid in digestion and tea made from comfrey is a natural decongestant.

The word cake comes from an old Teutonic word, kaka. The English used the diminutive form, koekje, to make the word cookie.

The Japanese have been researching a controversial treatment called aromatherapy. This therapy is based on the premise that certain scents can wipe away tension and fatigue and help us to relax. Among the scents that they have found to have relaxation benefits are: basil, its fresh smell has a hot and cold feel to the skin which is very comforting; camomile, used to reduce insomnia and stress; eucalyptus, its camphor like smell calms the nerves; lavender, a gentle pick-me-up; jasmine, known for centuries for its sensual properties.

3 eggs
2 teaspoons vanilla

Frosting:
1/2 cup butter
4 Tablespoons cocoa
6 Tablespoons milk <u>or</u> half and half
1/2 teaspoon vanilla
1 pound box of powdered sugar

> Preheat oven to 350°. Prepare two 9 inch cake pans.
> Heat chocolate and a little butter in saucepan over low heat, stirring constantly, until melted and smooth. Cool thoroughly.
> Stir sour cream into the chocolate.
> Mix in flour, soda, salt and baking powder.
> Cream butter and gradually beat in sugars until light and fluffy. Add eggs, one at a time, mixing well as you add each one.
> Alternatively add sour cream mixture and flour mixture to eggs and sugar. Blend well. Add vanilla.
> Pour into pans and bake for 35 to 40 minutes or until center springs back when touched.
> Cool in pans for 10 minutes then remove and complete cooling on racks.
> Blend all frosting ingredients together, adding more milk if needed to make it spreadable. Spread frosting on cake.

Pavlova

Pavlova is an Aussie dessert. Bill homesteaded in Australia for a few years, so this is one of his favorites. This is a natural for us because we often use Hollandaise at the inn. The contrast of flavors and textures in this dish is always interesting.

4 egg whites, room temperature
1/2 teaspoon salt
1/4 teaspoons cream of tartar
1 cup fine granulated sugar
4 teaspoon cornstarch
2 teaspoons white wine vinegar
1 teaspoon pure vanilla
1 cup heavy cream, whipped
2-3 kiwis, peeled and sliced

>Preheat oven to 275°.
>Grease and flour a 10 inch springform cake pan.
>Place egg whites in mixer bowl with salt and cream of tartar. Beat until they hold stiff peaks.
>Add sugar, 1 heaping Tablespoon at a time, beating constantly until mixture is smooth and glossy. This takes 7-10 minutes.
>Beat in cornstarch, vinegar and vanilla.
>Pile gently into cake pan. Pile higher on sides to form a bowl.
>Bake in slow oven, 60 - 90 minutes. Bake until meringue is pale beige and firm. It will pull away from the sides of the pan.
>Whip cream just before serving and pile on Pavlova. Cover top with sliced kiwi.
>Serve at once.

Any ripe, sweet fruit can be used instead of kiwis on the Pavlova. My favorites are peaches, raspberries or strawberries. Use your favorite for variety.
-Susan

The little berries we call huckleberries are known as Bilberries in other parts of the world. Small, tart, and magenta colored, they often accompany meat and game dishes in Scandinavia.

We recommend moderation as opposed to martyrdom when it comes to the question of food and health. As gourmets we realize the importance of well prepared food and drink. As health conscious adults we know the importance of good nutrition. When we entertain we have found that a few simple substitutions will cut calories and fat without sacrificing the festive atmosphere.

For example: Four ounces of Champagne saves 251 calories and 16 grams of fat over an equal amount of egg nog. Many cheese shops now carry gourmet cheeses which can save you many calories over high fat Brie. Pretzels, grilled shrimp, pita wedges and fresh vegetables are also better nutrition choices.

Stilton or Roquefort Cookies

2 1/4 cups flour
1/2 cup powder sugar
1/2 teaspoon salt
1/2 teaspoon white pepper
1 cup butter
1 cup Stilton or Roquefort cheese
3 Tablespoons dry sherry
1 2/3 cups finely chopped, toasted walnuts

>Sift together dry ingredients. Cut in butter until mixture resembles corn meal.
>Add cheese and mix until blended.
>Sprinkle with sherry and 1 cup walnuts. Blend well and shape into logs about 9 inches long. Roll logs in remaining walnuts, pressing firmly into dough. Wrap in wax paper and chill well.
>Preheat oven to 400°.
>Cut dough into 1/4 inch slices. Place slices on a lightly greased cookie sheet and bake for 8 minutes or until lightly browned. Cool on wire racks.
>Serve with fruit, cheese and white wine.
Makes 3 dozen cookies.

Walnut Shortbread

2 cups soft butter
1 cup sugar
1 cup walnut pieces
2 teaspoons vanilla
1/4 teaspoon salt
4 cups sifted flour

>Preheat oven to 325°.
>Prepare 15 inch X 10 inch X 1 inch jelly roll pan, lightly grease sides and bottom.
>Grind walnuts to a coarse meal in food processor, blender or food grinder.
>Cream butter and sugar until light and fluffy.
>Beat the nuts, vanilla and salt into butter mixture. Add flour and mix well.
>Spoon the dough into pan and smooth it out to fill pan easily. The dough will not change shape as it cooks so level the top with a spatula so it will cook evenly.
>Bake 40-45 minutes until lightly browned.
>Cool in pan, then cut into bars.
Makes 75 - 1 inch X 2 inch bars.

Gardening is not only a tonic to the soul and soothing to the mind, but is an excellent workout as well, burning up to 500 calories an hour.

Nut Cookies

1 egg
1 cup dark brown sugar
5 Tablespoons flour
pinch baking soda
pinch salt
1 cup chopped walnuts
1/2 teaspoon vanilla

>Preheat oven to 325°.
>Beat egg. Stir in brown sugar, flour, soda and salt.
>Add nuts and vanilla.
>Pour into buttered 8 inch X 8 inch pan. Bake 30-40 minutes. Allow to cool in pan.
>Cut into squares.
Makes 16 - 2 inch squares.

**Maturity means reaquiring the seriousness one had as a child at play.
. . . Nietzsche**

A couple of marbles in the bottom of a double boiler will rattle when the water is low, reminding you to add more water before the pan burns.

When choosing a sweetener remember that sugar has less taste than honey. The new gourmet honeys often have very strong flavors.

-Susan

Chewy Chocolate Chip Bars

1/2 cup butter
1/2 cup firmly packed brown sugar
1 cup flour
2 eggs
1 cup firmly packed brown sugar
1 1/2 teaspoons vanilla
2 Tablespoons flour
1 teaspoon baking powder
1/2 teaspoon salt
1 cup finely chopped nuts
1 cup bittersweet chocolate chips

>Preheat oven to 350°.
>Mix the first three ingredients together.
>Pat into bottom of a greased 9 inch X 13 inch pan.
>Bake for 10 minutes. Cool.
>Beat together the remaining ingredients, keeping the chocolate chips aside.
>Spread the mixture over the first layer and sprinkle chocolate chips over the top.
>Bake at 350° for 25 minutes or until lightly browned.
>Cool, then cut into bars.

Makes 24 bars.

Ginger Spice Cookies

1 1/2 cups butter
2 cups brown sugar
1/2 cup molasses
4 cups flour
1 cup rolled oats
2 eggs

2 teaspoons ginger
2 teaspoons cinnamon
4 teaspoons soda
1/2 teaspoon salt
1/2 cup currants or raisins
3/4 cup chopped nuts

> Preheat oven to 375°.
> Blend butter, sugar, and molasses in the bowl of a food processor. Add eggs, one at a time until thoroughly incorporated.
> Add flour, soda, and spices and pulse until all the flour has been absorbed.
> Put dough into a mixing bowl and blend in oats, nuts, and currants, using a wooden spoon or spatula. Drop by heaping teaspoonfuls onto a buttered cookie sheet.
> Bake for 12 to 15 minutes or until nicely browned.

Little Chocolate Melts

1 cup butter
1/4 cup sugar
2 cups unsifted flour
1 cup (6 ounces) semi-sweet or milk chocolate chips

> Preheat oven to 350°.
> Cream butter and sugar in a medium bowl until light.
> Gradually add flour, then stir in chocolate chips.
> Roll rounded teaspoons of dough into balls and place on an unbuttered cookie sheet. Bake for 12 to 14 minutes. Cookies will be pale.

The best way to melt chocolate is over a very low heat in the top of a double boiler over hot water. If you add a little butter when you melt the chocolate, it will help prevent burning the chocolate and also makes it easier to clean the pan afterwards.

Ignorance doesn't kill you, but it makes you sweat a lot.
. . . Haitian Proverb

If the juice spills over when baking a fruit pie, just shake a little salt into the spills. It will cause the spill to burn to a crisp so that it can be easily scraped off with a spatula.
- Susan

> Let stand for a couple of minutes before removing. Lightly dust with powdered sugar if desired.

Chocolate - Espresso Mousse

4 ounces semisweet chocolate *or*
3/4 cup chocolate chips
1/2 cup butter
1/4 cup strong espresso
6 Tablespoons sugar
3 large eggs

>Over low heat in a small heavy saucepan, melt the chocolate with the espresso.
>While chocolate is melting, cut the butter into small pieces and put it in the bowl of a food processor fitted with a metal blade. Process the butter with the sugar until fluffy, about 1 minute.
>Add warm melted chocolate-espresso mixture. Process 15 seconds. Scrape sides of bowl and process for another 20 seconds.
>Add eggs, one at a time, and process for 15 seconds with each egg addition.
>Divide the mousse into individual serving dishes and refrigerate until well chilled, at least 4 hours.

Serves 4-6.

Double Berry Tart

I have used fresh raspberries, blueberries or blackberries in this recipe with equal success, but any fresh fruit such as peaches or nectarines should work as well.

1/4 cup butter
1/4 cup brown sugar
1 1/2 cups flour
1/2 teaspoon vanilla
1/4 cup buttermilk
1/2 cup chopped nuts (walnuts, pecans, or hazelnuts)
8 ounces cream cheese
2 Tablespoons sour cream
1 teaspoon vanilla
2 Tablespoons sugar
5 cups fresh berries
1/2 cup water
1/2 cup orange juice
1/2 cup sugar
2 Tablespoons corn starch

> Preheat oven to 375°.
> Blend together butter, brown sugar, flour, vanilla, buttermilk, and nuts until they resemble coarse meal.
> Turn the crumbs into a buttered 10 inch tart pan with a removable bottom.
> Press the crumbs firmly over the bottom and up the sides. Chill the shell for 30 minutes.
> Bake the shell for 15-20 minutes or until golden brown.
> Remove from the oven and let cool.
> Cream together the cream cheese, sour cream, vanilla and 2 Tablespoons sugar. Spread the mixture over the cooled shell.

Favorite Liqueurs

Curacao is an inexpensive orange flavored liqueur.

Cointreau and **Triple Sec** are also orange flavored but a bit more expensive.

Fraise is a French liqueur from strawberries.

Framboise is also from France but made from raspberries. It is a very strong flavored liqueur.

Calvados is a French apple brandy.

Applejack is the American version which is not as rich bodied.

Tia Maria and **Kahlua** are coffee flavored liqueurs.

Cassis is made from currants.

Creme de Cocoa is chocolate flavored, while

Creme de Menthe has a very minty taste.

Sambuca has a wonderful anise flavor and is usually served with three coffee beans in the bottom of the glass for luck.

After a good dinner, one can forgive anybody, even one's own relatives.
- Oscar Wilde

> In a sauce pan, blend 3 cups of the berries, water, orange juice, 1/2 cup sugar and corn starch.
> Gently cook over medium heat until the mixture thickens and clears.
> Gently pour the berries over the cheese filling. While this mixture is still warm, but not hot, spread two additional cups of berries that have not been cooked on top of the berries that have been cooked and distribute evenly.
> Chill at least a couple of hours before serving.

Luscious Lemon Dessert

When this dessert is finished it is layered with the custard on the bottom and the soufflé on the top. It can be served with a sprinkling of fresh berries as a garnish.

1/2 cup unsalted butter, softened
1 1/2 cups sugar
6 large eggs, at room temperature
2/3 cup fresh lemon juice
zest of the lemons used to make the juice, minced
2/3 cup flour
3 cups half & half
1/2 teaspoon salt

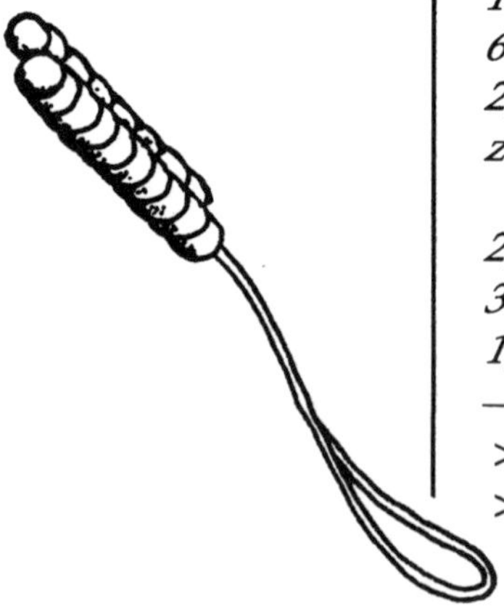

>Pre-heat oven to 350°.
>In a food processor with a metal blade, cream together the butter and the sugar until the mixture is light and fluffy.
>Separate eggs. Add the yolks one at a time to the butter and sugar mixture, beating well after each addition.

>Beat in lemon juice, zest and flour. Stir in half & half and blend until well combined.
>In a separate bowl, beat the egg whites with the salt until they hold soft peaks. Be sure not to over-beat.
>Fold 1/4 of the whites into the lemon mixture until lightened. Then gently fold in the remainder until blended.
>Pour batter into a lightly buttered 9 inch round cake pan. Put this pan into a larger pan and fill the larger pan with water until it reaches half way up the cake pan.
>Bake in the middle of the oven for 45 - 60 minutes or until the top is golden and the custard is set. Let it cool slightly. Serve warm.
Serves 4.

Strawberries Supreme

The sauce in this recipe is also good over a slice of Angel Food cake. Lemon juice and lemon rind may be substituted for the orange juice and rind.

2 cup strawberries, washed, hulled, cut in half
1 Tablespoon sugar
1/2 cup sugar
2 teaspoons grated orange rind
1/2 cup orange juice
1 cup heavy cream, whipped

>Put strawberries in a small bowl and sprinkle with 1 Tablespoon sugar.
>In a small saucepan, combine the 1/2 cup sugar, orange juice and orange rind and bring to a boil. Stir until the sugar dis-

Forget injuries. Never forget kindness.
- Confucius

solves, then gently simmer without stirring for 10 minutes. Let cool completely.

>At serving time, whip the cream and fold it into the orange syrup.

>Put the berries into individual serving bowls and top with a generous spoonful of orange cream.

Serves 4.

A sherbet and a sorbet are basically the same thing, but most sherbets have a little milk or egg white added to the fruit purée. Ices are fruit juice, sweetener and water frozen in an ice cream machine. They are generally more watery than a sorbet. Frapeé is a fruit sherbet frozen hard and pressed through a strainer when it is slightly thawed to give it a slushy texture. Ice cream is smooth because it contains a high perecntage of butter fat. Vanilla ice cream must have at least 10% butterfat and chocolate must have 8% butterfat to qualify as an ice cream by the FDA. If it has less than that it is called ice milk.

A wine sorbet can be used between courses as a palate cleanser.

Fresh Fruit Sorbet

I have made this sorbet with a large variety of fruits and it has always been delicious. Pick whatever is plentiful and ripe.

1 - 2 quarts of fresh fruit
sugar or honey to taste
2 Tablespoons lemon juice
fruit liqueur

>Freeze fruit. Do not freeze solid. If your fruit is frozen solid, allow it to thaw a bit before processing.

>In a food processor fitted with a metal blade, purée the fruit in small batches at a time, adding sugar or honey to taste. Between each batch empty purée into a bowl.

>After all of the fruit is processed, taste and sweeten to your palate.

>Add 2 Tablespoons lemon juice and any fruit liqueur you like as an additional flavor enhancer, but do not over do.

>Freeze again. 30 minutes before serving remove from freezer to soften. Just prior to serving purée again.

Ice Cream Torte

1 package Angel Flake coconut, sweetened
1 cup almonds, blanched and finely chopped
2 eggs whites
1 quart chocolate ice cream, softened
1 quart coffee ice cream, softened
fudge sauce
1 crushed toffee candy bar

>Preheat oven to 350°.
>Butter bottom of a 10 inch springform pan.
>Beat egg whites until soft peaks form.
>Fold coconut and almonds into egg whites. Line bottom of pan with the mixture.
>Bake until lightly browned. Let cool.
>Empty the quart of softened chocolate ice cream on top of crust, spreading smoothly. Freeze briefly.
>Coat with fudge sauce. Add the quart of coffee ice cream to the layers and top with the remainder of the fudge sauce.
>Sprinkle with chopped toffee candy and freeze at least 4 hours or until firm.

Fudge Sauce

1/2 stick butter
3/4 cocoa powder, unsweetened, Droste <u>or</u> Hershey
1/2 cup golden brown sugar
1/2 cup half and half
2 Tablespoons corn syrup
1 teaspoon vanilla

>Heat all ingredients, except vanilla, together over medium high heat until sauce reaches rolling boil.

There are a few foods which are so nutritious that they help make up for other nutritional lapses. Try to work the following into your diet over a week's time to help keep your diet balanced:

Broccoli
Brussel Sprouts
Cabbage
Cantaloupe
Carrots
Dark Greens
Dried Beans
Non-fat Milk
Non-fat Yogurt
Whole grain cereals
Salmon
Sweet Potatoes
Citrus Fruits
Multi-grained Bread

>Remove from heat and add vanilla.
>Allow to cool slightly before layering on ice cream torte, according to directions above.

Crème fraîche is a heavy cultured cream. It has been thickened and allowed to develop a delicate sour taste, giving it a tart edge. It has a variety of uses; it can be dolloped over dessert and berries, added to sauces for richness, or spooned over vegetables as a simple sauce. Because it can be cooked without fear of separation, it has greater versatility than sour cream. It also can be stored in the refrigerator for up to two weeks.

Crème Fraîche

1 cup heavy cream (not ultra pasteurized)
1 cup dairy sour cream

>Whisk the two creams together in a bowl.
>Cover the bowl and let stand in a warm place overnight.
>Place in a covered container and refrigerate for at least 8 hours. The longer the mixture remains in the refrigerator, the tarter the flavor. The creme fraiche should be quite thick.

Conversion Chart

ounces to grams - multiply ounce figure by 28.3
grams to ounces - multiply gram figure by .0353
pounds to grams - multiply pound figure 453.59
pounds to kilograms - multiply pound figure by 0.45
ounces to milliliters - multiply ounce figure by 30
cups to liters - multiply cup figure by 0.24
Fahrenheit to Celsius - subtract 32 from Fahrenheit, multiply by 5, then divide by 9
Celsius to Fahrenheit - multiply Celsius figure by 9, divide by 5, then add 32

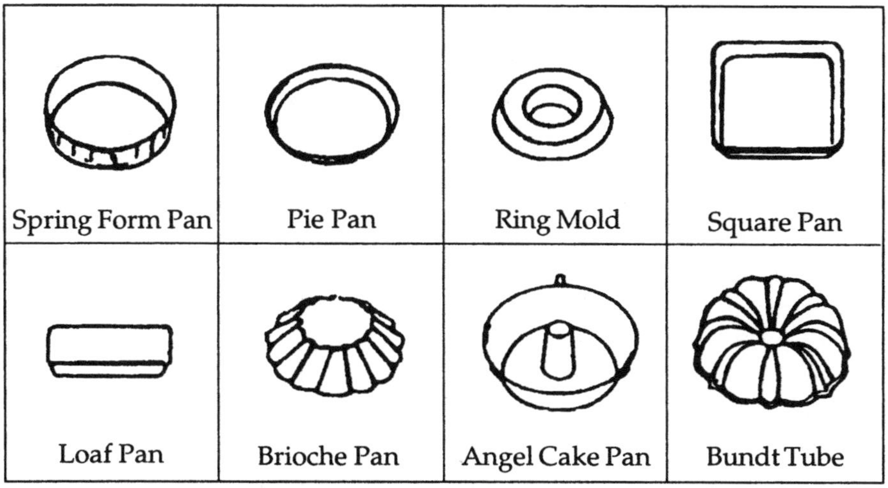

Total Volume of Pans

9" x 3 1/2" Bundt Tube - 9 cups
9" x 3 1/2" Angel Cake - 12 cups
8" x 3" Spring Form - 12 cups
9" x 3" Spring Form - 16 cups
8 1/2" x 2 1/4" ring mold - 4 ½ cups
9 1/4" x 2 3/4" ring mold - 8 cups
9 1/2" x 3 1/4" Brioche - 8 cups

Turtleback Facts

Turtleback Farm Inn is a country inn located on Orcas Island, considered by most to be the loveliest of the islands that dot the San Juan archipelago in the sparkling waters of Puget Sound. The inn overlooks eighty acres of forest and farmland in the shadow of Turtleback Mountain (discernible from the ferry that brings passengers from Friday Harbor). It commands a spectacular view of lush meadows, duck ponds and outbuildings with Mt. Constitution providing the backdrop to the east.

The inn is centrally located in beautiful Crow Valley, 6 miles from the ferry landing and close to Moran State Park. There are many recreational activities on the island; golfing, wind surfing, sea kayaking, moped and bicycle rentals, fresh water fishing and swimming in the park, charter boats for saltwater fishing, cruising and sailing, fascinating artisans and shops, and many excellent restaurants. Bill and Susan Fletcher, the proprietors, will be happy to help in the planning of your activities.

Orcas Island is accessible by ferries from Anacortes and Victoria, B.C., or by Kenmore Air.

Reservations should be made well ahead for the inn is often booked weeks in advance. Room rates are based on double occupancy and all rooms have a private bath. Rates vary seasonally. Breakfast for two is included in the price of the room. Because of the rural nature of Turtleback Farm, the inn cannot accept pets. Children are accepted by special arrangement only.

For further information about the inn or to make reservations please call or write:

Turtleback Farm Inn
1981 Crow Valley Road
Eastsound, WA 98245
(800) 376-4914 ❖ (360) 376-4914
www.turtlebackinn.com

Index

BISCOTTI
Twice Baked Cookies

Bill and I have a morning ritual. I usually go up to the Inn early to prepare breakfast. Bill will start his day looking after the animals and property. I am up, showered and dressed while Bill makes a great latte which we share with a biscotti. We certainly enjoy these crunchy treats with the coffee that give a jump start to our morning.

2 cups sugar
1 cup butter or margarine melted
1/4 cup anise seeds
1/4 cup Amaretto or other anise flavored liqueur
3 Tbs. bourbon or 3 Tbs. vanilla + 1 Tbs. water
6 eggs
5-7 cups flour
1 Tbs. baking powder
2 cups coarsely chopped almonds

> Melt butter and add sugar, anise seeds, liqueur and bourbon (or vanilla + water). Beat in eggs, one at a time. Mix flour and baking powder, then add to egg mixture. Add nuts and stir thoroughly. Batter should not be sticky but should hold its shape. Place in buttered bowl and let rest in refrigerator 2 – 3 hours.

> Pre-heat oven to 375. Grease two baking sheets and shape dough directly onto these sheets, making two flat loaves 1/2 ″ thick, 2″ wide and as long as the sheet. Place loaves parallel and well apart. Bake 20 minutes or until lightly browned.

> Remove from oven and let loaves cool to the touch on the baking sheets. Cut each loaf into diagonal slices 1/2″ to 3/4″ thick.

> Place cookies close together, cut side down on the baking sheets and re-bake in 375 oven for 15 minutes or until lightly toasted. Cool on wire rack until cold. Store in airtight containers.

Banana Breakfast Souffle

6 Bananas
3 Tbs. dark brown sugar
6 eggs separated
1 tsp salt
1 Cup milk
2 tsp. Vanilla
1 Tbs. dark rum or bourbon
1 Cup flour
8 Tbs. (1/4 lb.) butter
1/4 Cup sugar
1/2 Cup pecan halves toasted

> Preheat oven to 375. Melt butter in a 12" non-stick, oven-proof fry pan. Pour 6 tablespoons into blender. In the remaining butter, melt the brown sugar. Cut 2 bananas diagonally about 1/4 inch thick and sauté in butter/sugar mixture until just coated and warm. Set pan off heat and remove banana slices.

> In the blender add milk, eggs yolks, vanilla, rum or bourbon and 4 bananas. Blend until bananas are pureed and then flour and blend again. In a large bowl, beat 6 egg whites with salt until they begin to hold soft peaks. Slowly add sugar and beat until white hold stiff peaks. Gently fold banana mixture into egg whites. Pour into prepared pan, top with banana slices and toasted nuts and bake in oven until puffed and golden – 25 to 30 minutes. Cut into slices, top with a drizzle of maple syrup and serve on warm plates with bacon or ham. Serves 6-8.

Savory Torte

For years we have offered our *Smoked Salmon Torte* for breakfast. This has been a very popular and requested recipe blending a smoked salmon filling with buckwheat crepes that are stacked 6 high. This recipe offers a new flavor combination and can be served for breakfast or luncheon.

Egg Crepes;

1 cup milk
1 cup unbleached white flour
4 eggs
2 TBS melted butter
pinch salt

> Mix the crepe ingredients well in a blender and let batter sit. The batter should resemble heavy cream. Heat a 10" skillet over medium high heat. I use a silverstone, sloping sided saute pan. Add 1/2 tsp. butter to pan before you make your first crepe. After the initial crepe is cooked, you should not need to add more butter. While tilting the pan. Add just enough batter to thinly cover the bottom of the pan. Cook until bubbles pop, about 1 minute. Turn over and brown the other side. This recipe should make 6 large crepes.

Filling

1 bunch spinach, cleaned, stemmed and chopped or 10 ounces frozen chopped spinach
1/2 pound mushrooms chopped
2 TBS butter
8 ounces cream cheese
pinch salt
grind of pepper
1/4/tsp. nutmeg

> Saute spinach and mushrooms in butter until tender and most of the moisture has evaporated. Add cream cheese and seasonings and mix well. Season to taste. Keep warm.

> Place a large recrtangle of foil on counter. Cook one crepe and place in middle of foil. Spread 20% of filling over crepe and top with second crepe. Repeat until you have 5 crepes covered with spinach/ mushroom mixture. Top with final crepe and seal in foil. Place in pre-heated 350 oven for a few minutes to be sure the torte is evenly warm. Cut into 8 wedges and serve with a dollop of sour cream and snipped chives or a few snipped green onion tops. (For a more subtantial meal, chopped and sauted ham can be added to the filling. I usually serve meat on the side as not all our guests eat meat.

Olive and Ham Loaf

2 cups all purpose flour
2 1/2 tsp.baking powder
1/2 cup dry white wine
1/2 cup dry vermouth
4 large eggs beaten
1/4 cup mild flavored olive oil
1/2 cup melted butter or margarine
1 1/2 cups finely diced cooked ham
1 1/2 cups grated raw milk cheddar or gruyere cheese
1 1/2 cups pitted and chopped black or green olives or a mixture of both

---

> Preheat oven to 350. Sift flour with baking powder into a large bowl. Make a well in the center and add wine, vermouth and eggs. Mix gently until just incorporated. Add oil and butter a few spoonfuls at a time mixing until you have a smooth dough. Add the remaining ingredients and blend.

> Grease with pan preparation (page 42) a 8″x 4″ loaf pan and add batter. Bake until loaf is golden brown and a toothpick inserted into the center comes out clean, about 55 minutes. Cool briefly on wire rack, then invert and cool. Serve with eggs for a very complete breakfast.

Fish on the Grill

Much of the Pacific Northwest is bordered or surrounded by water. We are fortunate to have a bountiful supply of fresh fish year round. Not all is locally caught but with the speed of delivery, fresh fish arrives almost daily. As a result, we eat a lot of fish usually simple prepared on the grill or in the broiler. A few tips might help you enjoy the goodness of well prepared fish.

---

1. *Cook relatively slowly after allowing the coals to burn down. This will seal in the juices. Ahi tuna is the only one we cook briefly over high heat.*

2. Brush grill with a light coating of oil to avoid sticking. A cut potato rubbed over the hot grill will also act as a lubricant.
3. Keep skin on when cooking and start with this side up. This will hold the piece together and the heat will draw the juices from the skin to the fish below. Turn the piece only once so as not to cause the piece to break.
4. Do not over season. We often use a mixture of an equal part of crushed garlic and crushed ginger mixed with 1 Tbs. sesame oil. I rub this on both sides of the fish and splash with a bit of lemon juice
5. When Bill prepares salmon, he often coats the flesh side with mayonnaise and a sprinkle of dill weed. Quick, easy and tasty.
6. If you are using your broiler instead of a bar-b-que, place the empty broiler pan under the heat and pre-heat hot before you put the fish on. This will seal in the juices and eliminate the need to turn the fish as it will be cooked quickly on both sides.

We use this approach with salmon, swordfish, halibut and most all meaty firm fish. Delicate fish such as sole, I usually do on the stove with a bit of olive oil and butter to cook. When done, I deglaze the pan with either vermouth or white wine and add some capers. This I pour over the fish and serve.

Pasta with Ham & Mushroom Sauce

This sauce is a tasty change from tomato based pasta sauces. We often use this with angel hair or capellini.

1/2 lb Porcini mushrooms, coarsely chopped
1 1/2 cup ham cup into 1/4 in. strips
2 T shallots, finely chopped
4 T butter
1 cup water
3/4 tsp. Italian herbs or basil
1 tsp. salt
1 cup whipping cream

> Melt butter in sauté pan. Cook shallots until soft then add mushrooms. Cook until mushrooms begin to color then add ham, water

and salt. Cook until liquid has almost evaporated, add cream cooking until cream has thickened a bit. Remove from heat and reserve.

Béchamel Sauce

1 1/2 cup milk, warmed
3 T butter
2 T flour
1/4 tsp. salt

> In a sauté pan, melt butter. Stir in flour and stir continuously until flour has been incorporated. Slowly stir in warmed milk and salt. Cook until thickened. Fold in ham-mushroom mixture. Keep warm.
> Cook pasta of choice. On warmed plates, pile paste and top with sauce. Sprinkle with freshly grated parmesan cheese.
> Serve with a tossed green salad and plenty of warm crusty bread.

Portobello Purses

1/4 C butter
1 Portobello mushroom - diced
1/2 C yellow onion - minced
1 T shallot - minced
1/4 C sherry
1/4 C ground walnuts
salt and pepper to taste
1 pkg. Filo pastry sheets
melted butter (enough to coat filo sheets)

> In a large skillet, heat butter to medium high and saute the mushroom, onion and shallot with the salt and pepper until the mixture becomes translucent, (approx. 4-5 minutes.) Watch carefully so these ingredients do not scorch. Add sherry and ground walnuts, reduce heat and simmer until liquid is almost evaporated. Let cool to room temperature.
> On a clean surface, lay 1 filo sheet and brush it with melted butter. Top with a second sheet and brush also with butter.

Repeat again so you have a stack of three buttered sheets. Cut into 2″ squares. Spoon a little mushroom mixture onto the middle of each square. Grab the four corners of a square, pull them together and pinch them closed, forming a purse. Brush a little butter on the outside of each purse and bake at 375° until golden brown.

Cranberry Chutney

A couple of years ago, Bill and I were driving home from Oregon and had the good fortune to stop in the cranberry growing area of the state. The cranberries had recently been harvested and we were delighted to bring home 20 pounds of fresh berries. We used some right away to make this recipe and the Apple-Cranberry Pie, and froze the rest. We enjoyed a cranberry chutney with dinner while on our trip. This recipe is my creation to duplicate what we had with our meal.

---

4 cups fresh or frozen cranberries
2 cups apples, cored and chopped
1 cup onion, chopped
1 cup raisins or currants
1 cup pecans, chopped
3 Tbs. minced, peeled fresh ginger
1 clove minced garlic
2 cups packed brown sugar
1/2 cup tarragon vinegar
1/2 tsp cloves
1/2 tsp. cinnamon
1/2 tsp. allspice
1/4 tsp. cayenne pepper
1 cup orange or cranberry juice

> Combine all the ingredients in a heavy, non-reactive saucepan and bring to boil, stirring constantly. Reduce heat to low and simmer for about 20 minutes. Stir occasionally. Store in glass or plastic jars. Keeps for a long time in the refrigerator.

Brownie Pie

Often many of us find ourselves with last minute family or friends for dinner. The following provides a tasty and certainly quick solution for dessert.

---

2 eggs
1 cup sugar
1/2 cup butter softened
1/2 cup flour
pinch salt
4 TBS cocoa
1/2 tsp. instant coffee granules
1 tsp. vanilla
1/2 cup chopped walnuts

> Preheat oven to 325. Grease and flour an 8" pie plate.

> Place all the ingredients except for the walnuts in the bowl of a food processor. Blend 2 minutes scraping down bowl a couple of times. Add nuts and pulse a couple of times to incorporate. Pour into pie plate and bake 30 minutes or until done. Like a meringue, pie will settle when cool. Cut into wedges and serve with either vanilla or coffee ice cream or whipped cream. If you have neither on hand, this is good alone.

Apple-Cranberry Pie

---

1 1/2 cup cranberries (fresh or thawed frozen)
1 1/4 cup sugar
1/4 cup currants or raisins soaked until plump in
1/4 cup brandy
6 T flour
3/4 tsp. cinnamon
1/2 tsp. nutmeg
1/4 tsp. salt
5-6 apples (about 2 1/4 lb.) pealed and sliced pastry for 9-10 in. single crust pie (page 64) baked blind for 10-12min.

Topping:

3/4 cup flour
1/2 cup firmly packed brown sugar
1/2 cup butter, cut into chunks

> Preheat oven 375.
> In a small bowl, mix 3/4 cup flour and brown sugar. Cut in butter with a pastry blender or hands until mixture is in small lumps. Set aside.
> Sort cranberries and discard any bruised or decaying ones. Rinse and drain.
> In a large bowl, mix 1 1/4 cup sugar, 6 T flour, cinnamon, nutmeg and salt. Lift currants from brandy with a slotted spoon and save brandy. Add cranberries, currants and apples to flour mixture and mix well. Pour filling into partially baked pie shell. Drizzle evenly with reserved brandy. Sprinkle reserved topping over top of cranberry filling.
> Put pie dish on a cookie sheet lined with foil. Bake on the bottom rack until apples are cooked and juices are bubbly. Be careful not to over cook crust edges. If browning too quickly, cover loosely with foil.
> Cook pie until warm. Serve with a scoop of vanilla or apple ice cream.

Dutch Cookies

1 cup sugar

1/2 Cup butter
1/2 Cup Crisco or other solid shortening
1 egg yolk
2 Cups flour
1 tsp. cinnamon
1/2 tsp. vanilla
Pinch salt
1 egg white diluted with 2 Tbs. water
3/4 Cup chopped nuts

> Preheat oven to 350. Butter the bottom of a 12"x 15" rimmed baking pan. In a food processor; cream butter, shortening, sugar and egg yolk. Add sifted flour, cinnamon, salt and vanilla and pulse until blended. Press evenly into the bottom of the baking pan. Brush with egg white mixture and sprinkle with nuts. Bake for 20 minutes. Cut into squares while warm.

Ginger Cakes with Molten Chocolate Centers

These tasty cakes are baked in 2-cup custard cups and inverted onto the dessert plate at serving time. Garnish with a dollop of whipped cream or vanilla ice cream.

Note: If you do not want to prepare your own fudge, you can use store-bought thick fudge sauce with success.

Cake

1 cup brown sugar, firmly packed
1/2 cup butter
1/2 cup molasses
2 cups flour
2 teaspoons ground ginger
1 1/2 teaspoon baking powder
1/2 teaspoon baking soda
Pinch salt
1 lightly beaten egg
1/2 cup warm milk

Ingredients - Chocolate Fudge for Center:

4 Tablespoons butter
1 cup light cream
2 cups sugar
2 ounces grated chocolate
1/8 teaspoon salt
1 teaspoon vanilla

> Cake: Preheat oven to 325 degrees. Grease and flour 6 custard cups; set aside. Combine sugar, butter, and molasses in small pan and cook over very low heat until butter is melted and sugar is dissolved; cool. Sift together into mixing bowl flour, ginger, baking powder, baking soda, and salt. Make well in center of dry ingredients and add cooked butter mixture; blend. Add milk and egg; beat about 3 minutes and pour into prepared cups.

> Bake cakes in preheated oven until the cakes begin to set, about 15 minutes. Drop 1 1/2 Tablespoons fudge mixture into center and continue baking until done. About 10-15 minutes more. Center will be molten so test the outside of the cakes. Loosen and invert on dessert plates or serve in cups they were baked in.

Did You Have to Borrow This Copy of the Turtleback Farm Inn Cookbook?

If you would like to have your own copy of this wonderful cookbook or perhaps purchase a few as gifts, we have included the simple order form below.

$16.95 Turtleback Farm Inn Cookbook

__________ Total for books
__________ Postage & Handling ($2.00 per book)
plus sales tax when applicable
__________ TOTAL

- -

Please Print:

Name ______________________________

Address ______________________________

____

City ______________ State ____ Zip Code ______

Mail Your Check or Money Order To:

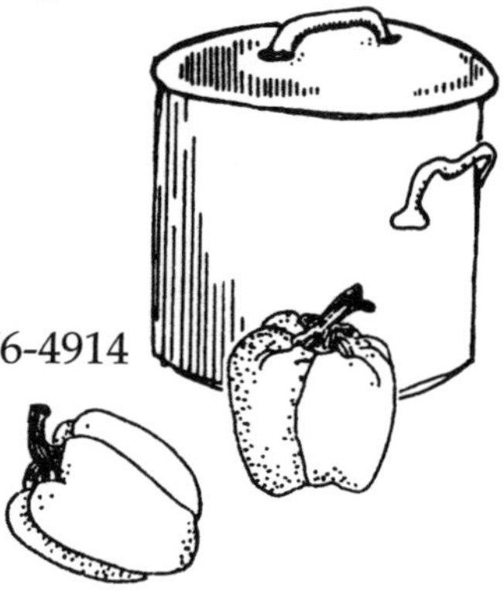

Turtleback Farm Inn
1981 Crow Valley Road
Eastsound, WA 98245
(800) 376-4914 ❖ (360) 376-4914
www.turtlebackinn.com